MW01230018

Homecoming

Troy Tartarini

Homecoming © 2023 Troy Tartarini

Presentation by *BookLeaf Publishing*

Web: www.bookleafpub.com

E-mail: info@bookleafpub.com

ISBN: 9789358314762

First edition 2023

1

Life has always had this weird sense of timing. For most of my life, I guess for as long as I can remember, I've had a crush on this girl from my town. It happened instantly on the day I first saw her. She stole a piece of my heart that day without even knowing it and I've been infatuated with her ever since. We were always drawn to each other, always hanging out with the same friends, but unfortunately we never had good timing.

She would always have a boyfriend when I was single and when she was single I always happened to have a girlfriend. We spent every party growing up sitting next to whoever we were dating at the time while we stared at one another all night long. There was something between us and I think we both knew it. We just never had the chance to give it a real shot.

We both had too much integrity to ever see if we would be anything. I think that is why I'm so drawn to her. Even if we had boyfriends or girlfriends and spent the entirety of our night staring at one another, we were still loyal. As much as we've both been craving to see what we had between us, we never got a chance to give it a real try. It's just something we chalked up to as bad timing. That was until the infamous tailgate at ZooMass.

It was going to be the biggest tailgate at the school ever. Everyone and their grandmothers were coming to this tailgate. Apparently, it was like the school's fiftieth homecoming or something and all of my friends were there ready to celebrate the new school year. They were all going into their sophomore year and the only other times I have ever visited Umass before was to help my brother move into school way back when. The guy was like a modern day Van Wilder.

On the other hand, I didn't go to college. I went to a tech school. You'll be able to tell by my grammatical errors and elementary vocabulary. I wound up going straight to work after high school and my college experience was strictly limited to the weekends. I would always bounce from college to college, weekend after weekend, visiting friends and living it up.

My brother, on the other hand, did five years at the Zoo. While my friends were freshmen at his school, he was out there buying them all the alcohol they needed while he finished the last semester of school. Now the time of the tailgate, it was his first year removed from the school so this was his tailgate. Apparently it was this big deal and in a way he felt obligated to go. Everyone who had ever gone to the school in the past five years was planning on coming back. Everyone that ever went to school there was filling their dorms like a can of sardines with their friends so they could spend the night. The school even enforced a limit of two guests per person to keep the numbers under control. Even the one hotel on campus was completely booked. You couldn't buy a place to sleep that night. It was that big of a deal.

Needless to say, both he and I were itching to get back to Zoomass. There wasn't going to be a better time than now for us to visit his old stomping grounds while all of my friends were there too. Umass was one of the few schools around the state that I haven't been able to party at yet. I was there to move my brother into college but never to party. I feel like I can't truly say I've been there until I've spent a Saturday there. This whole homecoming thing was the perfect chance to pop my cherry.

David and I decided we were going to go to the tailgate that Friday night the day before.

Better late than never, right? He had found out all his old roommates were making it a point to get back to Zoomass that year for the tailgate. Once he heard that he was ready to go. I was with him that night as things developed and I knew I had to be there too. All my friends were there. She went to school there which meant there was a chance I could run into her. He looked at me and didn't even have to say any words. I just nodded my head yes and just like that we were committed to visiting the Zoo in the morning.

"The only thing you gotta do is find a place to sleep." That was the one stipulation I had to deal with. My brother was fortunate to find a room with one of his friends at the hotel. They weren't sure if there was going to be enough for me so I was on my own.

"That's fine, I'll figure it out." I mean most of my friends went to school there. They lived there in the dorms. I'm sure someone had to have space for one more. All I've been waiting for has been an excuse for me to get out there and see everyone. There was no better time than this. My brother was offering to drive us out there for the biggest homecoming Umass has ever seen. There was no way I was going to let the lack of a place to sleep keep me from seeing the Zoo.

4

"I'm gonna see if Steven wants to come with us too." He was one of our friends. Well, I guess I should say more of my brother's friend than mine but we all hang out together. I was friends with his younger brother who was my age, one of my best friends truthfully speaking. Matt was exactly who I was going to ask about some extra lodging for our visit. He's been one of my best friends forever so I was optimistic he was going to have a spot for me.

It was all a spur of the moment kind of thing by us but somehow as soon as we started making moves, things started going our way. My brother asked Steven and he was all game for it. So there we were the night before, with our departure about eight hours away. We woke up that morning eager, loaded my brother's car up, picked up Steven and headed for Zoomass.

It was just shy of a two hour ride for us. We made it a point to leave early enough so we could be there for when the first beers of the day were cracked.

It was the middle of October and it couldn't have been a better time to be driving through the sticks of Massachusetts. Each of us spent the entire drive admiring the beautiful foliage, bumping some of our favorite songs, and mentally prepped ourselves for the tailgate.

We didn't stop the whole way there. The only time we stopped was at the first packie we saw off the highway. I was still underage so had to wait in the car. Twenty is the most pointless age to be. They came out with a thirty rack, some twisted teas, and a sleeve of nips for us to start with. We all sucked down a nip each to give us enough energy to finish the rest of the drive.

Our first stop was the hotel. It was where my brother was staying and all his friends were meeting. My brother put the car in park, shut it off, and got out of it all in one motion and headed to the trunk. He was clearly ready to party. He ripped open the case and handed each of us a beer. "Alright guys, here's to the Zoo." We cracked the beers and all stood by his car in the hotel parking lot, sharing our first beers together before we went inside. Steven texted his brother Matt to let him know we were here and to see what he was doing.

"Matt and his friends are just waking up. They're about to get started." Steven filled us in, we finished our beers, and headed inside. This tiny hotel. It looked like it was only about four floors high, maybe twenty rooms a floor, no wonder why they filled up so quickly.

The hotel felt like it was inspired by the Shinning. It had the same wallpaper walls, had this creepy receptionist checking us in, and creepy old pictures of old guys on the walls. I was kind of glad there wasn't any room for me in this haunted hotel.

Walking down the hallway I could feel my phone vibrate. It was a text from Matt, "Tyler can't wait to see you, we'll meet up at the tailgate."

"Hell yeah, I couldn't wait to see my dude." I was too excited to answer. Just as I was putting my phone into my pocket he texted me again, "Did you hear who's single?" Before he even gave me a chance to answer he wrote back, "Alex."

My heart dropped. Alex was the girl from our town that I've had the biggest crush on. Matt knows it. Evidently this is going to be the first time we're both single at the same time. I couldn't wait to see her out and be able to do more than just stare at her from across the party. I only hoped that I'd get to see her out tonight. It's been a long time coming.

I had no idea what to say to Matt. I didn't even know what I was feeling at the moment. All I was able to type was, "Matt, I'll see you soon."

David broke me from my state of nirvana when he said, "Alright guys, let's go." as he opened the door to the hotel room. Just like that our tailgate officially started.

2

Steven and I followed David's lead inside. As I was walking into the hotel room I saw the bed and thought to myself, "Where the hell am I going to be sleeping tonight?" Steven was the only one with a definitive place to sleep; with his brother. Which reminded me that I forgot to ask him if I could stay with him too. He was here hoping that his friend still had a bed for him later in one of their rooms.

Once I snapped out of my head and noticed how packed this hotel room was, I forgot about me not having a place to sleep. That was a later issue. It was party time now. It didn't seem like anyone was worried about where they were going to sleep tonight. Our day was just getting started. The room was filled with all of my brother's friends from school. I didn't know any of them. I had no idea what we were getting into.

Almost instantly Steven and I lost my brother in the hotel room. He knew the first few people at the door and stopped to catch up with them. He's been bouncing around talking to everyone that has been funneling in. It was kind of weird for me to see, but it was like some of his friends saw him on this pedestal like he was some sort of Zoomass legend. Everyone was waiting to say hi to him. Steven recognized someone from the last time he visited so I posted by myself, grabbed another beer from the case David was holding, and found an empty spot by the window to post up.

There were about twenty-five people slammed inside this hotel room. I have never been to a dorm party. I have never been to a hotel party before. In just fifteen minutes of leaning on the window sill embracing the scene in front of me, I realized at that exact moment how intoxicating college truly was.

There was almost a pound of weed sitting on the table in the hotel room with five packs of grape garcia wraps lying next to it waiting to be rolled. I didn't even know there was a bathroom in their room until a group of five or six people periodically funneled out from there to join the rest of us in the room. Each one of them walked out of that bathroom sniffing and wiping their noses. Everything I assumed college to be like was right. I've been missing out on some of the biggest parties of our lives. College would be a blast.

"You've never been up here before, have you?" I heard Steven's comforting voice break me from my daze.

"No actually. I was here once to help him move in his freshman year, but I haven't been here since. I've never been to a school this big before." I found the college lifestyle compelling. It's wild for me to think that for four years they let us kids live unsupervised like this. People live on their own with little to no responsibilities and barely any supervision. I could only imagine what I would find myself getting into if I went to college.

"Yeah this is Umass, it's exactly how I remember it to be. Even if it's been a couple years since I've last been out here. Things haven't really changed much."

"I can only imagine doing this for four years." I was in awe, I was envious, I couldn't believe all the things I had been missing out on by going straight to work after high school. Like I said I've visited friends in school before, but just here in the hotel room, I've seen more things than I have at any other school. I'm a stoner and never seen a pound of weed before until the Zoo and honestly haven't seen it once since. While I've been busting my ass at work, it seems like they're just out here finding every excuse to party. I was so ready to jump on their train. I figured if I'm going to be hanging out with so many Umass alumni I might as well go all the way with it. You know what they say when in Rome. "This is exciting, today's going to be a good day."

"Without a doubt. I'll text Matt and see if he's left the dorms yet." Steven was stoic. He didn't look like a kid in the candy store like I did at this party. He was calm, cool, and confident while he was leaning on the wall talking to me. Being part of the "younger brother clan" we had growing up, he was the one we all idolized. He was the epitome of cool to us.

"Did you hear?" I know he hasn't. I just need to talk to someone about it, "I guess Alex is single…" I paused for a second to cover my mouth because I started smiling way too much, "I'm hoping we get to cross paths with her tonight." I then proceeded to fill Steven in on this little crush I've had on her that has been developing over the years.

"See you said it, today's going to be a great day." Steven smiled while he said that. That solidified it, we were going to have an incredible day.

3

We didn't spend too much time in the hotel room. Most of these people had got here the night before so had a later start to their days than we did. We got here early enough to still catch them at the hotel so we could slug back a couple beers before we all herded like cattle to the tailgate. I didn't go to school there so I didn't know my way around, but I knew where I was going that day. It felt like everyone that was on campus was walking in one direction. Everyone and literally their mothers were there that day. We jay walked over main street, cut through some side streets, and found our way into the EAC. just like they did in Finding Nemo.

There were cops on horses at every intersection making sure that none of us left the paths that were dictated for us to walk. Like dogs with their animals on the farm, they keep us flowing towards the tailgate. They had no issue with us drinking, they didn't care if we were carrying racks of beers in our hands, or if someone lit up a blunt for their walk. All they cared about was that we kept it moving. The walk from the hotel to the tailgate was long enough for us to finish our beers and throw them away by the time we got there.

I couldn't believe how many people were already down there partying. I turned around to see how many more people were still coming behind us and I swear it had to be the entire school. Walking down the hill towards the parking lot that was hosting the tailgate I could see about fifteen lanes of cars trapped inside. The alleys in between where cars normally would be driving up and down looking for a spot, were completely filled with people just standing holding red solo cups.

It was nine forty-five in the morning, and people were full throttle. As soon as I stepped into that parking lot I could see thousands of people smiling in the prime time of fall in New England, it was on. As far as I could tell we were late to the party. The first guy at the entrance of the parking lot was sitting in the back of his truck bragging about how dope of a spot he got at six in the morning. I was convinced this was the biggest day the school had ever had. Everybody who's anybody showed up. I, on the other hand, was only concerned about one person showing up... Alex. I had my fingers crossed that I would see her.

Of course I was excited to see Matt and the rest of my friends too. They were the reason why I made the decision to come out here in the first place. I only found out about Alex when I got here. It's been months since I've seen him and we were going to reunite with our brothers and friends and his school friends at the tailgate. It was going to be legen... wait for it...dary.

We were steps from the tailgate and I became anxious. (I was more ignorant back then) We stepped out of line for just a moment to fuel up and crack another beer for the walk to wherever we were going. My brother was texting his friends, while Steven was on the phone with Matt trying to figure out which lane they were in so we could finally drop all these beers and have a home base. I just wish someone was able to capture that moment of me and my brother slugging back a couple beers with the cops right behind us. As long as we were sipping from our cans or solo cups they didn't care. You just better make damn sure you weren't caught drinking out of any glass. That seemed to be the only thing they cared about. If they saw you drinking a bottle they would pounce on you and toss you in the back of the paddle wagon for the remainder of the tailgate. Not a place you wanted to end up this early in the day or at all.

"Guys he's this way." Steven pointed vaguely in a direction deeper into the crowd and we started following him. David picked up our thirty rack and we were off into the heart of the tailgate. "He said he's over by the J sign."

None of us knew what we were looking for. We only knew where to go and to look for them chilling in the back of a truck. I think every car in that lane, on both sides, was a pickup truck. Every single one of them was jam-packed with sports jerseys, crop tops, kegs, and a cloud of marijuana smoke hovered over the entire parking lot. It felt like I was in heaven. Everyone was shoulder to shoulder and there was zero room to walk. We literally had to push our way through the crowd of people to get to where we wanted.

We took the path of least resistance and walked through every group of girls that was in our way. We were walking aimlessly looking for Matt. I was so far caught up with this experience and everything going on around me that I wouldn't have even noticed Matt or any of my friends unless they slapped me in the face. I was lost in the Zoo. I couldn't believe it and it was barely 10 am. Fortunately, all I had to do was to follow David, who was following Steven, serpentining through the crowd.

Somehow over the crowd of people yelling and chanting nonsense, Steven heard his brother Matt call out his name from a distance like it was some sort of brother telepathy. Instantly we all B-lined it to whoever's truck Matt was yelling from. He hopped down from the truck and met us before we got there. Everyone in the truck had turned their head to see where he was going. Matt is a celebrity wherever he goes. Everyone knew him and he knew everyone. He was the king of our friend groups. It didn't take long for him to claim his crown with his friends at Umass. He met us in the middle of the aisle, greeting each of us with a hug as he always does.

"I'm so happy you guys are here." Matt was overwhelmed with excitement. As were all of us, I was so happy to be with him again. It's been way overdue since we've last seen each other. There I was following another one of us family members but this time it was Matt not Steven who led the way back to the truck. On the way back to the truck he somehow managed to make more friends and say hi to everyone we walked by. He was like an A-list celebrity around here just as he was back home.

When we finally got to the truck, after who knows who I met, there were way too many

17

names for me to remember. David dropped our case of beer and handed us each another round. "Alright here we go, let's have a day, boys." David gave us a short pep talk with a smile and it was real, we were at the tailgate.

My brother got caught up talking to this girl that bumped into him so Steven and I hopped into the back of the truck where some of Matt's college friends were sitting. Steven and I said hi to them and then sat along the railings of the truck bed observing the crowd. There had to be eight of us comfortably chilling in the back of the truck, soaking up the fall air, drinking the day away with some good company and maybe thousands of people squeezing into this parking lot. It was going to be perfect.

4

After I finished my fourth beer of the morning it was time for me to break the seal. A little prematurely in the day considering it wasn't even noon yet but I couldn't hold it anymore. I let Steven know where I was going and headed into the wildness of the parking lot known as the Zoo. Again I had to push myself through the crowd, following the same tactic I learnt earlier, choosing the path of least resistance, serpentining through the groups of girls in the crowd, saying excuse me as I passed through them.

I was shocked when I saw how long the line at the bathroom already was. Evidently I wasn't the only rookie breaking the seal so early. There had to be a hundred of us waiting for a porter john to open up. There was no discrepancy between guys or girls porter johns, it was a free-for-all. There was no line either, there was just all of us waiting for our chance to step to the front and be next. There were about two dozen of them shitters lined up at the end of the parking lot for us all to share. I just felt terrible for the girls, I know what it can be like inside some of those things and

I pray that we can keep a few of them at least half decent inside there for them to use.

It took about ten minutes for me to get remotely close to the front of the line. For a while there I couldn't even see the porter john but now that I could see it, I could feel my piss getting ready to bust out. It was getting harder and harder to hold it in as I kept on getting closer and closer to the front of the line.

I wasn't the only one ready to explode. Two guys started walking to the same shitter after someone came out. One dude said to the other one wicked confrontationally, "Dude back off it's my turn I've been waiting." Then the taller dude, the other guy started yelling, talking about how the short dude cut him and came from another line, "You're in that line go wait over there." The other guy didn't take it well and I remember thinking, "Here we go."

They started off by just shoving one another but it quickly escalated after that. They started throwing punches and squared up to fight each other in the bathroom line at eleven thirty in the morning. In the midst of these fools fighting, the girl that was next in line, only two people in front of me, seized the moment to occupy the vacant porter john and emptied her tank. I must have been the only person to notice her pull it off. I was looking around and it seemed like everyone's eyes were fixated on the fight. Hell, the horse cops didn't even notice the fight until it was almost over. This girl pulled off the greatest move, I only hope that it wasn't too dirty in there.

If you ask me, a fight this early in the day is a lose-lose kind of situation. They fought over what, taking a piss. Now one of them is in pain covered in blood and piss, while the other punched his ticket with an early entrance to the back of the paddy wagon. Who will inevitably wind up pissing himself because once you're in the paddy wagon there's no coming out until it's filled and they get back to the police station.

Once the chaos of the fight had settled I found myself unscathed next in line for the bathroom. I claimed the next urinal making sure no one was racing me for it. I did my business and got out of there quickly. The bathroom line was not a place I wanted to go back to. As I was walking out I could hear two other guys arguing in the distance at the other end of the bathroom line and I just walked away. I wasn't ready to see another fight. Next time I have to go to the bathroom I'm walking the other way to the woods and finding myself a nice tree to water.

It took me almost fifteen minutes to find the truck everyone was chilling at. I still couldn't wrap my head around how many people were still funneling into this parking lot. It was everything I expected college to be like. There were guys shotgunning beer, girls giving out body shots, and some of the dopest sports jerseys filled the aisles of the tailgate. If you wanted to talk to someone who wasn't directly adjacent to you, you had to scream at the top of your lungs to be heard. This place was a shit show and I couldn't help but think to myself, "This is why they call it the Zoo." I was starting to love it.

"Tyler." I could hear Matt calling out my name from a distance. His voice comforted me and was my beacon to find my way back to the truck. I wasn't that comfortable yet to be alone in the Zoo. Truthfully speaking, this whole thing kind of intimated me. I heard him ask me "Want a mixie?" as I was climbing back into the tailgate but never even gave me a chance to answer and started pouring a solo cup for me.

My lack of college experience was going to cripple me. It wasn't even high noon yet and we're already starting with the mixies. I was still underage, this whole drinking thing was new to me. I was a lightweight for sure, but this was Umass. There were no rules here, there were no excuses, just party. I couldn't say no. I'd sound like such a pussy if I said, "Nah thank you I'm good on the mixie, I'm just gonna stick to beer today thank you." Matt knew I wouldn't say no and promptly filled my hand with a mixie.

"Have you met any of these guys yet?" Matt asked me about his new friends that showed up while I was gone but their names slipped my mind. This was the most amount of people I have ever seen in one spot before. Our spot seemed to be the spot to be. The truck was packed with guys, booze, and boobs, I mean girls. Our crew wasn't just limited to the truck. Our crew started taking over the entire J aisle. I felt like Matt kept on introducing me to all these new people telling me who they are, expecting me to retain it all.

"Are these all your friends?" I was baffled that he knew all these people by name and their story. He wasn't just saying hi to these people, he was genuinely talking with them.

"Yeah, they're some of my friends out here. They just stopped by to say hi. I think they're parked over in lot A." I couldn't believe this one group of girls he introduced me to were all his friends. I have never in my life stood that close to nor have I ever been in the presence of so many attractive girls that closely before. Matt introduced me to them and then them to me telling me each of their names and them mine. It was nice and said I was glad to meet them but still couldn't remember any of their names. I wasn't involved in the conversation. I didn't care about meeting them and moved on from the group. As of a couple hours ago, there was only one person I wanted to meet.

"A couple of those girls thought you were cute. I had told them some of my friends from back home were coming and you intrigued them. Where'd you go?" That was one of the many things that made Matt such a good friend, he is always looking out for his friends, hoping to bring people together, even when none of us ever ask him. The world's greatest wingman.

"Really, did they say something? I honestly didn't even notice." I paused for a second to build up enough courage to ask, "Did you hear anything from Alex?" I wouldn't know if a girl was hitting on me unless she grabbed my cheeks and kissed me first. I'm so oblivious to all that; I'm terrible when it comes to flirting with girls, which today worked out for me since my only concern was Alex. I have no idea what or if anything will transpire between us but I needed to know. I just needed to try.

It was impossible for the man in me not to notice the plethora of beautiful girls that came out for the tailgate. Maybe it's my twenty-year-old testosterone speaking but I've never been in a one spot that was filled with such incredible-looking girls. I had to find Alex. I needed to find out where we stood together because if there's no chance between us I can't hang onto false hope anymore.

5

While Matt was talking to his friends, I got lost in another day's dream thinking about Alex. Honestly, I haven't been able to stop thinking about her ever since I found out that I may actually have a chance with her. I've been reminiscing on all those close calls we had, all those intimate moments we shared, hoping that today would be the day they would all add up and amount to something.

David again broke me from my daydream and asked me, "Yo Tyler I'm walking over to F lane to meet some friends, do you want to come or stay here?"

"I think I'm gonna stay here, you can take the beer if you want. Matt is making me mixies now." Regardless if Alex showed up or not I came here to see Matt and all his friends here. I wanted to get the Zoomass experience firsthand as if this was just another Saturday for me at Umass. I already saw what some of the alumni were doing and knew I had to learn to walk before I could run with the kids my age. She wasn't going to dictate my day.

"Alright cool. I'm gonna leave the beers here then. Just make sure they stay under the truck in the shade so they don't warm up in the sun. I feel like this should go without saying but no one takes a beer without permission." He hopped out of the truck and vanished into the crowd as I replaced him in the truck. I planted myself right above the beers in the shade just as my brother was making sure no one found our secret stash.

Being elevated and looking out on the tailgate from this perspective painted a clearer picture of how popular our parking spot was. From sitting in the bed of the truck looking out into the sea of people around us, it was like we were the epicenter of the whole thing. Matt knew everybody and everybody seemed to be flowing this way.

"Tyler, do you mind passing me another beer?" After David left, the responsibility of the beers was up to me. I became the King Of The Bud Lights. He told me he wanted to make sure no one took one, I didn't know I was responsible for dishing them out too. Steven was in on this rack with us, he got a beer every time he asked. He wasn't someone I wasn't going to give a beer to considering he paid for more of this beer than I did. I'm not old enough to buy my own drinks.

Once Steven cracked his beer and picked up his mixie with his other hand, people noticed him. One of the guys in the back of the truck called him out for double-fisting drinks in the bed of the truck, got himself another beer from his own case, and let out this loud cheer, "To homecoming!" He raised his beer, chugged one of them, and we all followed his lead out of respect and chugged our beers. I felt like I was floating on cloud nine sitting there with all these people drinking on such a beautiful day. It all just felt surreal.

I then felt Matt tap me on the shoulder, "How you doing, do you want another mixie?" It ran in the family, both him and Steven always made us feel comfortable in any and every situation. I was too far away from Steven to talk to him and had barely made any conversation with the people next to me or anyone at that point until Matt came over to me.

"No I'm good…" and out of the purest and lamest form of desperation, I asked him again, "Is Alex coming?"

"She said she may stop by…" It wasn't what I wanted to hear, "I think her and her friends are a couple rows down." Matt could see this sadness take over my face and quickly picked me back up, "But she did say she was going to come out with us tonight. Don't worry, you'll get a chance to see her."

As quickly as my face was overcome with anguish, it was relieved by his settling words that put a smile back on my face. It was all I needed to hear. I just wanted to have a chance with her. We've missed so many chances back in the day, we are destined to have at least one moment together. I know it. I just need to get a chance with her.

6

It was like there was wave after wave of people coming to our truck to talk to Matt. He was like an A-list celebrity around here. The aisle our truck was in was jam-packed. Hell, the whole parking lot was filled with more people than I have ever seen in one place and it felt like everyone was coming to see him. I had found a safe place in the back of the truck and enjoyed the more laid-back atmosphere. I wasn't overwhelmed by the amount of people smashing shoulders with each other to say hi to Matt. I was in the back of the truck with the boys. We were good.

I was loving just sitting there people-watching. There was this one group of his lax bros friends that came by to share a drink with us and I wasn't sure if they planned it or not but they were all dressed the same. Following them, another group of their friends that lived on the floor below arrived, carrying a backpack full of jello shots for everyone. They all came there to say hi to Matt. Him being the affectionate kind-hearted person he was, made it a point to say hi to all of his friends that came by. I had no issue with chilling in the back of the truck with everyone else and most importantly where the beer was. It was an ideal day to be chilling outside.

But when another group of girls came by to say hi to him, he called for me from the truck to come over, then turned back around to talk to the girls. When I got over there he introduced me to the three of them, just like he had with the group earlier. He told me each of their names as he introduced them thinking I was retaining all this information. I thought the last group of girls were some of the most attractive girls I have ever seen. These three girls gave me three reasons why I was wrong. I was barely able to introduce myself, forgetting my train of thought each time I locked eyes with one of them.

Before our small talk ended I said something stupid as my brother came back from his friend's tailgate. He was eager for another beer and was now in full Alumni mode. I said my goodbyes to these girls who weren't Alex and ran over to hear why my brother was laughing so hard.

"Guys it's wild out there, there are a shit ton of cops on horses shitting all over the place. When I was walking back I saw someone looking at their phone while they were walking and stepped ankle-deep into a pile of horse shit. He looked like he was gonna puke when he realized what he stepped in."

We all started laughing along with him. Obviously we felt bad for the guy, I mean that would ruin my day, but we were a group of friends that seldom saw any good luck. So seeing someone else share the same misfortune as we typically do will always be comical.

"What are your friends doing for the game?" Matt came over and asked David and it didn't make sense to me. What did they mean, what are they doing for the game?

I interrupted them, "Wait, are we not going to the game?" The stadium was literally right there. I could see it. I could probably throw a rock and hit the main entrance. I assumed the whole reason why we were here partying the way we were this early in the day was because they don't serve alcohol inside the stadium. We were just getting ready.

Both he and Matt shared a smile with each other as if they thought my ignorance was cute. Matt finally answered me after they shared their laugh, "No…" He chuckled again, "No one goes to the football games. We just come here as an excuse to darty. (My least favorite word ever) This was just how we were starting our day.

"I think they're going to the bar on the other side of the stadium. They said something about leaving the tailgate a little earlier to make sure they got in. I figured we might as well give that a try." David finally got around to answering Matt's question. He got pulled away to say hi to someone and I officially have no idea what's going on anymore. Apparently, we're not here to watch the football game we're tailgating. I was just along for the ride.

7

The kids whose truck it was we were tailgating at, finally had this brilliant idea to drop his tailgate so we had more seating for everyone. At least that's what I thought he dropped the tailgate for. We all started cheering, some guys even clapped and applauded him for his superior thinking. There were about eight of us sitting in the bed of the truck with the tailgate up, never once did any of us think about opening the bed of the truck to be more accommodating to the rest of the group.

Evidently it wasn't for extra seating. His tailgate was used strictly for the game flip cup. His truck bed was pristine… minus the alcohol stains from the game. The tailgate was lined flat so each inch of the tailgate could be used to flip your cup. He refused to let anyone plant their ass on his tailgate to rest or to sit down. He made it abundantly clear that his tailgate was made specifically for partying and today's game- flip cup.

He didn't want the brim of his cup landing right where someone had just farted or rested their pooper on his tailgate. He wanted his cups clean from any fecal matter. He even wiped the whole thing down before we played. He was the type of guy that had hand sanitizer clipped on his key chain.

"Let's go, we're all playing." He yelled from the bed of his truck. Like he was the King of our tailgate.

This was maybe the second time I have ever played flip cup. I didn't know much; I remembered the rules, and it was a perfect drinking game. When I first played we all stood around a table raced to chug our drinks and flip our cups before the other team. This time we were playing, we had no table, it was straight-up anarchy. His tailgate only had enough room for so many cups. It wasn't designed for a fifteen-on-fifteen game of flip cup. Some people made things more challenging for themselves by choosing to flip their cups on the rail of the truck bed, limiting the area they had to land. I for one am terrible at that game and thought those guys were being dicks showing off their skills. Others were so bad, like me, we were sharing spots on the tailgate so we had a real surface to flip our cups onto.

After one game I thought this whole thing was completely lawless. Promptly after our first two warm-up rounds, I concluded this was all out chaos. The teams were even, it was fifteen vs fifteen. We did the first couple of practice rounds with water, which I thought we were actually going to be playing with, but I was mistaken. We only used the water to preserve booze for when we played the real game. I know I couldn't handle a day of drinking like that.

Seeing them pour alcohol into their cups made me want to quit the game before it even started. Each one of them seemed to be going up against a friend or a foe or someone they've had this vendetta against. Not me, I was just the guy at the end of the line that joined the game because they needed another guy. I was the caboose; I was intimidated by everyone's confidence. I felt like I didn't fit in at all, and based on my past performance I know I'm not any good.

So I tried to use my inexperience and lack of skills as a cop-out to get out of the game, "Truthfully this is only like my second time playing this game. I don't think I'd help either team if I played." I whispered into Matt's ear, who was the only person I knew next to me, admitting I was scared to play. There was no way I was going to admit that out loud for everyone else to hear.

As he always does, Matt found the right words to say, "You're fine, just take the first shot during the game and ride it out. It's early. If you're not up for it we'll both quit so the teams stay fair." He didn't make much eye contact with me, in fact, he didn't make any eye contact with me, he was all business getting everyone set up for the game making sure everyone had a shot in their cup and knew where they were flipping their cups. This was for bragging rights for eternity. Whoever is victorious will always be able to look back and say, "Remember that time we won playing flip cup at the tailgate." I knew I at least owed him a couple games of flip cup to keep the teams even for a little while before I quit.

"I'm just saying don't judge me for my lack of ability, I know I suck at this game, like way worse than I am at beer pong." I was beyond nervous, I was petrified. I was intimidated by the people I had to flip cups against and was starting to psych myself out. I was two years behind all these kids when it came to party experience. These kids probably played flip cup on Thursday nights just so they had something to do. Me on the other hand might as well call this my first time playing.

Before we started the first game for real I attempted to lighten the mood a little bit, hoping to relax myself a little bit, cracking a joke with my opponent. I told her the same thing I said to Matt that I was wicked nervous in hopes that she would too make me feel more comfortable.

I was wrong. She didn't even give it a chance. She didn't care that I was nervous. I think it actually gave her some satisfaction knowing I was high-strung. All she said to me was, "Good then it sounds like I'll at least get a turn and chug to have this shot. I need it."

I feel like she had something going on and I was just on the receiving end of it. I had just admitted to her how nervous I was and there she goes making fun of me telling everyone on her team not to worry, they'll all be getting a turn because of me. Because she knew I wouldn't ever be able to flip a cup. She completely blew up my spot and truthfully I didn't want to play anymore.

Just as I was about to quit and walk away from the game, the two guys at the end of the truck had started the game. They raised their cups up, then down, then up, and down again to start the game. It was on and whether or not I liked it, I was a part of it. Just as quickly as it took for them to slug down their shots of vodka they flipped their cups on their first try like they were pros and yelled at the next guys simultaneously to go.

"Damn, these guys are good." The other girl across from me said under her breath. I must have been the only one that heard her because when she said that and saw me turn towards her with my face covered in fear, she put her head down and waited for her turn just as scared as I was. I talked myself into gaining some confidence thinking, maybe I won't be the worst one out here playing.

The next two guys both flipped their cups on the first try. It became evidently clear to me that I was nowhere close to their skill level at this game. In the back of my mind I was hoping that the next person sucked so bad that I wouldn't even get a chance to take my shot or flip my cup. Then at least that way for the next game I know I won't be the worst player. Plus I just started drinking alcohol in my life. I knew I had no tolerance for it and it wasn't even noon yet. If I wanted any chance of surviving all night the less shots the better.

The next two people flipped their cups on the first try again. The guys after them slowed the game down a little bit, taking a couple flips until they finally landed their cup. I was going next, at the same time as the girl who was talking shit about me before the game, it was on now.

"Fuck this is it." was the pep talk I gave myself in my head as I reached for my shot. I could see my brother in my peripherals intently watching me and this chick battle it out for the winner. He went early for the other team and could only wait to see who would get the first flip..

I refused to make any eye contact with him or my opponent. I might have been nervous but now that it was my turn it was all about winning. It was a switch that went off and all of a sudden we're not friends right now and honestly depending on how this goes I may never be friends with this person I'm facing. We were in the middle of a competition and the only thing that mattered was proving who the best flip cupper was at the tailgate.

This was my combine and I couldn't let my team down. I finished my drink before she did and gave it my first flip skeptical it was going to work. Just as she finished her drink my cup flipped onto its side. She went to flip her cup as I was grabbing mine and got it on the first try. I took my cup, gave it another flip and got it. I failed my team. I blocked out all the noise and filled my cup to start the next game.

Their victory was short-lived. As soon as we lost we claimed to make it a best-of-three series for all the bragging rights. I filled my cup with another shot ready for the next game. I gave a look over to David and Steven on the other team to let them know it's all business now.

The game started more intensely than the last one as both teams flipped their cups on their first try. The two that are next finished their drinks at the same time eyeing up their flip simultaneously. My teammate got it on his first flip. His opponent missed... big time. He flipped it off the tailgate.. While he was spending his time fetching his cup from under the truck, my teammate sipped and flipped their cup before he got his cup back on the table.

It was now my turn, with this newfound confidence of knowing that this girl still had to go after me, and a full person lead, I was eager to prove myself to my team. I slugged down whatever shot was in my cup and lined up my flip... Bang, first try. There was no time to celebrate getting it on my first flip. It was her turn now to seal the game.

Just as she proved in the first round she took the shot like a champ. We had a person lead still. With no pressure on her mind she flipped her cup and nailed it on her first flip. So did my next teammate and just like that we found ourselves onto game three. "The rubber match." It had just turned noon, and we all knew we had a long day ahead of us, we knew that if any of us wanted to make it out that night this needed to be our last game. Game three... this time it was my turn to start.

I eyed Steven and David just as I did before the last game started. This time we all nodded at each other understanding this was it. Best of luck, that was it, it was all business. I started the game against my opponent with the traditional up, down, up, down, chug, start and we were on our way. She finished her drink faster than I did, clearly more experienced than I was. By the time she was about ready to flip her cup, I was just finishing my chug and setting my cup on the tailgate. She flipped it on her first try. I could see it land perfectly as I was winding up to flip my cup. I instantly could feel the pressure fall heavier on me. It was my job to get our team off to a fast start. I got my finger under the cup and flicked it perfectly. First try again. Maybe a moment slower on the shot but the first flip is all that matters.

After that our team was perfect. The girl after me flipped it on the first try and it seemed to go like dominoes after that. We won by a landslide proving that the first game was a complete fluke. It was an epic win for all of us involved, and after the match, my ego boosted immensely. Or maybe it was the alcohol but either way I was riding this high horse. We won.

8

Then it hit me, it was finally time for me to piss again. After Matt and I finished celebrating our moment of victory I let him know I had to run to the bathroom to take care of business. I haven't left the truck since the last time I had to pee and I knew I wasn't going back to the Porter Johns. When I turned to leave our HQ it looked like the amount of people at the tailgate had doubled since I last looked around. I firmly believed that the entire college was here at the tailgate that day.

I was completely overwhelmed and became anxious with the amount of people there was behind me. I couldn't even turn around to leave without bumping into someone by accident. It felt like I was a bumper car maneuvering around the crowd to get to where I wanted to go.

When I got to the end of the aisle we were in all of the pedestrian traffic stopped. I don't know how or who gave this guy permission to just get up and leave in the middle of the tailgate but it was happening. I could see the cops on horses escorting him through the crowds clearing a path for him to leave. It brought a whole crowd to an abrupt stop that no one was ready for. I accidentally bumped into this girl in front of me spilling my drink all over the both of us. "Oh my God, I'm so sorry." I quickly pulled out my undershirt to use as a rag to help dry off some of my spills.

She grabbed my hand, stopping me from helping dry her off and comforted me, " Aww you're so cute, honestly don't worry about it, this place is a zoo. It's almost expected to happen here." I was baffled that she wasn't pissed at me. I mean she was incredibly attractive and I fully expected her to be kind of stuck up and react in a bitchy way because I spilt my drink on her. She was the polar opposite. She was wicked nice to me.

I was at a loss for words, I didn't anticipate her kindness. The truth just kind of came out, "I'm sorry I'm just trying to get to the bathroom."

"That's where we are coming from. We went to the woods, it's much quicker than the Porter Potty." I never really struck up a conversation with a girl like that before. I wasn't sure what the next step was but I knew I needed to get her name.

"Hey I'm Tyler, I'm just visiting my friend Matt." (a shot in the dark that she knew who Matt was) If I was a smoother talker, maybe just a tad bit more witty, I would have thought to ask her her name or open the door for more conversation. But it seemed like it was taking her a second to process that information.

"Wait, oh my God I love Matt, you're one of his friends visiting from back home right? Where are you guys tailgating? I'm Stacy by the way." As she finished talking the traffic jam settled and we started drifting from each other going separate ways. Stacy... one of the few names I've happened to remember in my life. Someone I wondered if I would ever see again.

I yelled over the crowd as she walked away for shits and giggles, "We're over in lot J." as if she heard me. I got out of the traffic jam and B-lined it straight towards the woods. I needed to go and I was not going back to the Porter Johns; it was not an option. Those things were dangerous and disgusting.

I followed the small crowd of people heading into the woods that were looking to water some trees as well. I made sure I went deep enough into the woods, far enough away from everyone, to ensure my Johnson stayed out of sight from anyone to make fun of.

I was deep in the woods, no one had any business coming out this far unless they were hoping to find some buried treasure or pot of gold.. I thought I was safe to pee but I was fastly mistaken. I could hear the leaves crinkle behind me like someone was walking towards me and my tree. I was frightened and had to see who was coming my way, accidentally peeing on my shoe, turning my head to peek. I figured I should finish my business first before I started looking up to see who was coming.

"Excuse me, do you think you could find another bush to use?" I was almost done. The least they could do was give me five more seconds.

"No, I like this tree right here. Thank you." It was a girl's voice... a familiar one, one that's warmed my heart before, and one that I'll always know. But the chances of her and I running into each other out here in the middle of the woods like this were improbable. Everyone we knew was over in lot J; there's no way Alex was here in the woods with me.

I rushed through my pee, shook my lunchbox dry, and turned around before I even had my pants all the way zipped up. That's when I turned around and saw exactly who I thought it was. Even knowing who was going to be there heckling me I was still astonished. I needed to say something but couldn't.

She was glowing so bright. With the woods as her backdrop she was looking like she was out there modeling. I was completely infatuated with her before that moment. Now seeing for the first time in almost a year, I knew I needed to talk to her, I needed her to say something before I started creeping her out staring at her the way I was. I just couldn't stop staring at her. She scurried off behind a tree to take care of business letting me gather my thoughts.

I've been dying to see her all day. As soon as I learnt that we were both single together. She has become my only priority since I got here. I couldn't just say nothing and let her walk away. As creepy as it sounds I waited on the path for her to finish. I mean I re-tied my shoes and took a couple hits of my one-hitter while she was finishing up. It was my turn to say something, anything, I couldn't be unheard. "Are you coming out with everyone tonight?" I did my best to play it cool but I know I was smiling like a teenager and my face was turning red. I just wanted to get a chance to talk with her, more than just seeing her at a mutual tree we decided to water.

"I was thinking about it…" She paused to smile at me in a way I can only think meant to tease me. She knows the feelings I have for her, she, at least I think she does seems to have the same ones. I mean staring at each other each time we're out has to amount to something.

She didn't want to give me a straight answer. The whole time she was downplaying coming out at night with us, smiling the whole time. I love her smile. It's been my favorite site to see for a while now. Then she continued on finishing her sentence, "… Some of my friends wanted to go to the football house after the game but I'm not sure what I'm doing yet."

Hearing that crushed me, it damn near broke my heart. Hearing she was going out elsewhere was a tough pill to swallow. If what I know about college continues to be correct, then I don't stand a chance with her at the football house. I had to keep it cool. I could let her know how devastating that was for me to hear. Regardless of how much of my heart she had, I knew it wasn't my time to tell her how I felt. I couldn't find anything else to say. I couldn't push the conversation any further, all I said was, "Alex I do hope to see you later, this would be one hell of a story to tell our kids one day."

I have no idea why I said that. I was doing my best to be confident and not let her know how much I was obsessed with her. I just knew the last thing I wanted to say to her was let me take you on a date but all I got out was, "I hope to see you later." A pathetic thing to say to anyone. I don't know if I thought I was being witty or it's something they would say in Californication but it just flowed out of me.

I thought I ruined the moment for us, but when she came back both witty and smooth I fell deeper for her, "Oh is this the story about how we first met? We're gonna tell our kids that I drank too much and couldn't hold in my bladder any longer and that I happened to piss next to the same tree as this guy I've known my whole life? We hit it off and never looked back? I will admit it's an original story. I can't say I've ever been hit on while I'm peeing in the woods. Who knows maybe one day I'll be telling our kids how I held your hair back while you puked this weekend too."

I was completely obsessed with her. Aside from her beauty, she always seems to be four steps ahead of me. Always being mean to me, teasing me, so seductively that it kept me falling for her more and more. "As long as we're talking to our kids I don't care what lie you come up with to tell them." It was like my inner Hank Moody took over and spoke for me.

"Maybe I'll see you later tonight." She finished peeing and left our tree with the biggest smile I've ever seen her have before. Bigger than I've ever seen her smile with one of her boyfriends, bigger than she does when she laughs at someone's jokes; she smiled big for me. I know her well enough to know that that smile wasn't like any of her others. I couldn't wait to see her again that night. She didn't say another word, she went back of into the words, towards the tailgate, before I could find anything to say.

More than before I was hoping that I would cross paths with her again that night. Or at least see her somewhere else besides the middle of the woods taking a piss.

9

I came out of those woods cheesing from cheek to cheek. If someone saw me glowing the way I was walking out they would have thought I just lost my virginity. The feeling, truthfully, wasn't far off. I was glowing. She had me on this high, I couldn't even walk straight. I was intoxicated with her now more than ever. I had to watch myself walk, making sure I was putting my left foot in front of my right, then back to the left then back to the right.

I was oblivious to everyone else that was running towards the woods to empty their tanks. I didn't know who any of them were. I didn't bother to look up at any of them, I didn't care to know who any of them were. I was so caught up dreaming about Alex, I didn't want to talk to anyone else for the moment. Our banter replayed in my head, her smile and her squinting eyes were all I could see. I desperately needed to see her again.

I got back to the crowd and was welcomed with a spray of form from someone cracking a beer on their head. I was unfazed. Alex was all I thought about lost in a daydream. Hearing the way she said my name repeats in my head, keeping me smiling through the crowd.

Matt again saw me walking up the aisle before I even saw him, yelled out my name, and waved me back over to our tailgate before I walked right past it. I heard my name and barreled through the crowd, pushing by the people I had to, to meet everyone hanging out around the truck. "You missed it, we finished the game without you. I'm sorry."

"That's fine." I didn't care much for that game anyway. I was hoping it was going to be defused by the time I came back. If I kept drinking at that rate I might find myself passed out before the sun even set and miss my one chance with Alex… No thanks. She still had me lost in nirvana. Apparently Matt was talking to me. I was preoccupied thinking about how mesmerizing Alex looked in the woods. I didn't even hear him talking to me. I think he could see it in my eyes.

"Tyler, you alright?" He knew I was out of it and I could hear he was genuinely concerned about me with his tone. David and Steven were facing the other way talking to a couple of friends but it was like both of their big brother sense kicked in. As soon as they heard Matt ask me if I was okay they turned around waiting for my answer.

"Yeah, no I'm fine.." I didn't know how to say it, "Guess who I just ran into." I still stood there smiling like a little kid waiting for his ice cream, or losing his virginity, knowing they would all be able to guess it on their first try.

It took a second but when it clicked with Matt he spoke immediately, "Wait, was it Alex?" He started smiling after he said it knowing he was right. I couldn't help but grin. He knew he was right.

"Yeah." I chuckled remembering how we had crossed paths, "We found each other watering the same bush out in the woods. Not at the same time of course, she got there just as I was pulling up my pants."

"I knew it, your smile gave it away." Matt always had a sixth sense for those things.

"Is she coming out with us tonight?" Steven was excited for me and wanted her to be coming out tonight with us for me. I filled him in on my crush on her and he was rooting for me. He said it earlier "Today's going to be a great day."

"I've got my fingers crossed for sure. She didn't say no and I definitely wasn't going to force it." I kept playing it cool in front of the guys but in reality she was setting off fireworks inside my heart that I was struggling to hide behind this little grin I was wearing. We had a moment out there, even if my pants were around my ankles.

I can only imagine how pathetic I must have looked standing there like that. I was so shocked to see her out in the woods of all places, but her smile was the most beautiful thing I've ever seen in this world. It's kind of ironic that we naturally met each other in nature of all places.

Man that smile though. When she smiles her eyes squint just enough so you can still see those two comforting brown eyes. Then she tries to cover her teeth with her hands as if to hide the fact that she's smiling. I think it's the cutest thing. She has no idea how beautiful she truly is. I was only wishing that I would be able to see her again and actually find the right words to finally tell her that.

10

There was a moment of silence amongst us. I was obviously too busy thinking about Alex, Matt was looking for his phone, and both of our brothers were on their phones placing some bets. It was a perfect silence in a way. None of us found it awkward. I think each of us found it blissful. Then finally Steven broke the ice, "Anyone want to go for a walk around this place before we run out of drinks?"

"Yeah."

"I'm down."

"Hell yeah, I'd love that."

"Alright, fill your cups, let's go." and just like that we ventured off into the uncharted tailgate. Matt, knowing this place and the people better than any of us, led the way and steered us away from the stadium to the back of the parking lot. It wasn't just our section but it was like the entire tailgate was chaotic. The cops didn't care if we were smoking or drinking just as long as we were being belligerent and were drinking out of glass. That seemed to be the only rule they implemented. As long as we followed those simple rules we were able to roam free, however we wanted.

My brother brought the few remaining beers we had left because he didn't trust anyone back at the truck to keep an eye on it. As long as he didn't flaunt our beer and carry it around like a jukebox we seemed to be in the clear.

Right after we made it out of our aisle, while we were sliding through the crowd, I smelt some people grilling. What a veteran move it was to actually bring a grill to a tailgate. I think they were the only ones who thought of that. And let me tell you, this wasn't the booze talking, but they were some of the best-smelling sausages my nose had ever smelt. My nose pinpointed who was the one cooking up those greasy sausages and was blown away by their setup.

These guys didn't just take up their parking spot, but the one next to them with it. Even though they only had one truck, they got here early enough to claim the spot adjacent to them to set up their grill and all of their chairs. They even had a tent "just in case" they had too much to drink and needed to sleep it off. Yeah a real tent, not one of those pop-up tents for the shade. It was just in the back of their truck waiting to be set up or for someone to ask them about it.

They were eager to show it off, I mistakenly made eye contact with the grill master and he waved me down with his thongs, inviting us over. I was in the back of our fun train and was in no position to steer it. I couldn't have met those people even if I wanted to. We walked by them without even flinching. All these things just started to feel normal. I guess at Umass weird is normal and normal is weird. It was starting to click for me, this is why people love the Zoo.

I gave my best shout from the back loud enough so someone could hear me over the crowd, "So really, no one goes to these games? I have never been to a football game before but this place seems electric. Why doesn't anyone go?" I couldn't believe that people came all the way out here just to pre-game the game.

I felt like my brother was ready to answer my question, "No one ever actually goes to the game." I guess no one seemed to care about going to the game and it baffled me. If no one goes to the games then I felt like we could sneak in there and sit at those empty seats in the first row on the fifty-yard line.

"I'd say maybe a quarter of these people here will make it into the stadium." Matt chimed in.

"Most of my friends are heading to the bar to keep drinking and watch the rest of the games this afternoon. All of the kids I knew on the team graduated. Plus this bar was where we used to always go." David was in his glory days. From what I could tell it must have been their place to go once they all became old enough to legally drink and apparently, it still is the place to go to.

"I'm pretty sure some of my friends are heading that way too." Matt solidified our plans for the game. There was just one issue though, I didn't have a fake ID. Matt was still nineteen but since being out here at school he's happened to get his hands on one of those fake IDs. I have not.

"Are you guys trying to head that way now?" Steven was just like me, ready to keep the day rolling, going with the flow. He was also a veteran at this whole bar thing and knew that it was better to get there sooner rather than later so we didn't have to wait in a line with the rest of the tailgate to get in.

I had to tell them, "Guys I hate to be that guy but I don't have a fake ID. I wouldn't be able to get into a bar."

"Ahh yeah, that's right, you never got a fake when we all did." Matt remembered asking me if I wanted one back then but I never felt the need for one. They all did it this past summer before they went to college but I was going to be the first to turn twenty-one and wasn't at college. I didn't care for one. They all got one because they had no way of getting alcohol out here. I always had someone that was able to do that for me. I never needed a fake ID until now.

"You can use mine. This place is going to be packed, they're barely going to be checking IDs." David seemed unfazed by this hiccup. "It's the only bar on campus and they'd be without business if they actually carded people and didn't let any of the fake IDs through."

We all laughed, sharing the moment of joy until reality set in. My brother was like 6' 5", and I barely even cracked six feet tall in my Dr. Martens. If they actually looked at his ID and compared it to me standing in front of them, there's no way it would work. "You're way taller than he is, there's no way that's going to work?" Steven could barely get it all out. Everything I was thinking. He kept on laughing at my brother's idea.

"Semantics guys, we'll be alright. Come on, we might as well head that way now. We got four beers left so we each got one for the road. I guess the plan will be when we get there I'll go in first while you guys just hang outside. Once I get in I'll come back outside to smoke a cigarette and give Tyler my ID for him to use."

That was our plan and we were going with it. We continued on our way again, serpentining through the crowd, making our way to the bar to beat the rush. The crowd was so drunk and oblivious at this point that David literally had to actually push people out of our way just so we could get through. "Excuse me" didn't work anymore. There was a lot of testosterone in the crowd, I was surprised we made it through everyone without getting in a fight or even an argument. The cops were patrolling the outside of the aisle strutting around on their horses more prominently now. They knew it was the beginning of the end and that everyone was heading over the hill into the land of drunken assholes.

I could see one of the horseback cops out of my peripherals eyeing us. In hopes of being proactive to avoid any further conflict, I tossed my half-drunk beer in the trash next to me and kept on walking by. I was in the back of the line, none of them would have known what I did or could give a shit for not finishing my beer. I was doing it for us. I was the only one of us without any proof that they could be legally drinking. I did not want me or any of us to end up in the back of the Paddy Wagon. They didn't notice it, I could feel it, one of the cops was staring at me right through his sunglasses. I felt like I was making eye contact with him. He pulled his horse to take a few strides to impede our path.

Once he crossed our path everyone else noticed him. None of us were doing anything wrong, the only ones who had a drink in their hands were old enough too. There was no reason for him to stop us the way he did. Hell, we weren't even the only ones drinking. While he had his horse gallop into our way he missed about twenty-five underage drinkers walking right by him with no issue. We just happened to be the ones this cop wanted to mess with.

We were in one of those wrong places, wrong time sort of thing. "You guys are going to throw that beer away right?" With his dark glasses on none of us could really tell who he was talking to.

He was up there sitting on his high horse looking down on us with his oversized aviators and we weren't even sure if he was talking to us.

David chugged the rest of his beer, it was all of our last beers, and came back at the cop, "Yeah I just finished it, I'm just looking for a trash barrel now." He wasn't being a dick back to the cop, okay, maybe he was a little bit, but he wasn't going to throw away his beer because the cop said so. It was going to be on his terms.

"There's one right over there." The cop didn't even break his death from looking down on us from his horse. All he did was nod his head in the direction of the trash that was twenty yards away. "Go ahead and throw out the rest of your guys' beers while you're at it." None of us argued anymore. Steven and Matt chugged the remaining beers and tossed them in the trash following David's lead. This wasn't our battle, not now.

Once everyone tossed their beer David boosted our morale and yelled right in front of the cop, "Alright guys let's head to the bar." giving us the last laugh. So to the bar we went.

11

I reflected for a moment, proud of myself, I survived the infamous tailgate. The clock was a quarter past one and I'm still going strong. A little buzzed, yeah at this point for sure but I kept on telling myself it's only because I haven't eaten yet. In the back of my mind lingered the daunting fact that I still had another twelve hours of drinking...at least. It didn't help that we were on our way to a bar on an empty stomach. My only hope was to chug a water or two and order myself some wings or fries to keep myself able to last all night.

It was a strange walk to the bar. I couldn't help but feel like we were amongst the fields of sheep being herded by the cops once again. They were essentially funneling us either to the one bar on campus David spoke of or back to the dorms. Each intersection we faced had more and more cops sitting on horses waiting for us. Pointing us in either direction. The only other time I see horses back in the city is during Christmas time but never a plethora like this. There had to be well over fifty horses patrolling the entire campus at this point. If my math is correct, I haven't started seeing double just yet.

They kept us walking fairly straight for the most part; the only treacherous part we faced was the uphill climb we had to take away from the tailgate. It was no issue coming there a few hours ago but now it is a different story. My legs were sore from standing most of the day and my calves were on fire walking up the hill. "Guys, my legs are killing me right now."

"I think I just now realized how out of shape I actually am. I'm sucking wind from just walking on an incline. I used to be an athlete." Steven was speaking for all of us, we were clearly well past our primes.

"Where is this bar anyway?" I was becoming severely parched and desperately needed a drink of any sort at this point.

"We're almost there, it's just past the top of this hill." I think David was the only person who actually knew where we were walking to. Matt was still learning his way around the school and if you dumped Steven or me in the middle of this campus neither of us would be able to navigate our way through it.

"I'm starting to sweat through my shirt." I was not having fun walking this much. I'm notoriously known as a bad sweater. So bad of a sweater that when I eat I sweat profusely it damn near looks like I just got out of the shower. When we reached the pinnacle of our climb I took a sigh of relief only to be faced at another intersection… Can you guess what was waiting for us at the top of the street?… more cops.

There they were again on their horses looking down at us like peasants. This intersection was slightly different. Instead of being forced to walk in one direction we finally had a choice to make. We had three options; we could go left back to the dorms and the cafeteria, or we could go right and through the school towards the hotel, or we could go straight and hit the one bar at the University. This seemed to be the end of the detour for these horse cops.

The path that led to the cafeteria was filled with people like me. All those underage kids who didn't have a fake ID and had to resort to going back to their dorm to party longer. Only the older alumni guys were walking back to the hotel. All those people had too far of a walk to go home this early so that left the rest of us marching straight to the bar. I was just following everyone else.

"Today's gonna be a long day of drinking isn't it?" I didn't say that to remind everyone else about the day we had in front of us. I only said it so I could mentally prepare myself for the rest of our day.

I started talking to myself inside my head, hyping myself up with some confidence saying; if they all order a beer I have to order a beer. I can't be the first one to drink water, nor can I let my first drink in my first bar be water. I had to keep up with the guys.

Matt subtly reminded me that not everyone can drink all day like this, "Some of my friends are going back to their dorms now to chill. I have a couple of other friends that went to nap and others that are at a house party already powering through it."

Somehow those words motivated me in a way to man up and order a beer, fuck water. However, my newfound confidence was going to be put on hold immediately as we came to a halt waiting in line of about twenty people looking to get into the bar.

We must have been maybe the third or fourth wave of people that left the tailgate early to flood the campus's only bar. David waited in line with us initially but wasn't really with us. He was using his height to look over every group of people in front of us in hopes that there was someone before us he knew so he could tag along and wait with them. Of course yeah he'd love to catch up on things with whoever he finds, but that wasn't why he was looking for someone. He needed them to get into the bar before us so he could come back out and give me his ID so I could sneak in. It was all part of his master plan.

And just like that he saw some old friends from school waiting about two groups back from the front of the line. "Alright, I'm gonna go jump in line with those guys over there. I guess you just stay back here waiting in line and I'll come back to give you the ID and smoke my cigarette until you all get inside." It was that simple. Operation Sneak Tyler into a bar was underway.

"You know, now that we're here and I can see the bouncer, I think this might actually work" Steven was being optimistic. As for me on the other hand I've never done anything like this before. Hell, I don't even know what the inside of a bar even looks like. I was shitting bricks nervous waiting in that line.

My mind was racing a million thoughts per second. I was wondering what would happen if we got caught, would we get thrown off campus, would we have to go wait in the back of the Paddy Wagon and wait with all those other drunk idiots from earlier until they filled it up? Would anyone bail me out? Who could I call? I was two hours and one hundred miles away from my self. I was terrified not because I was going into my first bar but because I was actually sneaking into a bar for the first time. The amount of people waiting to get into the bar was not helping my anxiety. It'd be so embarrassing to get kicked out in front of all these people. What if Alex sees me?

I decided to take my mind off it to search for my happy place. "Did you say Alex was coming out with us tonight?" She was the perfect segway. I'd much rather be talking about her rather than think about what would happen if we actually got caught sneaking into the bar.

Matt smiled before he answered, "She told me she was going to try and meet us out tonight. You guys must have really had a moment out there in the woods. I thought she had other plans tonight. I didn't think she was gonna come out with us but it seems like she is now."

"We did, or at least I think we did. I mean we'll see, right? Like if she comes out or not." I wasn't getting my hopes up. I'd believe it when I see it.

"You'll be alright Tyler, she'll come out tonight." Matt seemed confident that she was coming out with us. I guess she has told her friends otherwise, leaving me with hope.

"Time will tell right." Steven calmly spoke. He was right, it's out of my control right now. Time will tell. I actually stood up a little straighter after replaying his words in my head. All I can do is enjoy the day as it comes.

"I think there's going to be a big group of us going out tonight. That's not even including if David and Steven come out with us tonight. Or if they bring any friends. You're going to see her for sure, wherever we go will be the place to be. Look at our crew." Matt was more excited about the night than any of us were and his vibe was setting the tone. Since we were his guests for the night, he wanted to make sure that tonight was the best night we'd ever had. He was the only one out of our group of four that was still a student here. We were relying on him to steer us in the right direction for an ever-lasting night. .

"I don't think I've met all your friends yet Matt, will most of them be coming out with us tonight?" Steven, like me, had only met a couple of his friends back when he helped move Matt into his dorm but it wasn't anything more than that.

"Oh yeah, they'll be there. They're part of that big crew I was talking about. They're dying to meet all of you guys too. You guys have been a nice surprise for everyone."

"Honestly tonight's gonna be a blast, whether or not Alex makes it out with us tonight." I couldn't hold my breath waiting to hear if she was coming out with us or not. I wanted to enjoy the night with four of my best friends and that was all that mattered to me.

12

This was a completely new experience for me. It wasn't just that I was hanging out at my first college tailgate, but it was because I'd been able to enjoy it with my brother all day. Up until that day the only time I've ever hung out with my brother for this long before was at a Sunday dinner back when we were younger. We were stuck there together at that point. Neither of us could drive then so there was no escape from one another even if we wanted to. This was the first time since then that we were actually hanging out.

There was enough of an age gap between us where we were never able to go out for a drink together, but have always been close enough that he would buy me booze for the weekend if I needed it. Plus most of our friends knew both of us so it was only a matter of time until we started hanging out together.

I guess I was just thinking about him a little more since he's been gone for a while now. Normally I wouldn't do anything like sneaking into a bar like this. I was a goodie-goodie. I did my best to stay out of trouble. I would go home to chill before I would attempt to sneak into a bar, but out here is a different world. Out here sneaking into a bar is a way of passage.

David's voice came from behind me startling me, "Ahh, what's up guys?" like he was Bugs Bunny. He had a cigarette in his mouth and was feeling around in his pockets looking for a lighter. Once he found it, he pulled it out, with his ID, and passed it over to me.

It was go time and I was ready to sneak into my first bar. "You'll be good, he's just glancing over IDs at the door," David said enough to make me feel confident and comfortable to sneak in.

"How is it in there? Is it crowded?" Matt wanted to get a feel for how it was inside since he was already suffering from FOMO from not being inside.

"I met those guys in Boston before, right." Steven thought he recognized one of the guys David cut the line to get in.

"Yeah, they came out with us to the bars after the Bruins game. And Yeah it's starting to get pretty crowded in there. There's no way all these people waiting in line are gonna get in…" He paused for a second, forgetting that we were still waiting in line to get in. "You guys should be good though, you're close enough to the front, you'll get in," David said; maybe he was speaking from experience. He's proved to have that Amherst instinct. "It's kind of a hilarious scene in there though, all the guys are around the bar betting on all the football games while all the girls are in the back of the place dancing or eating at tables."

My eyes lit up. I created this whole little illusion in my head about what I was going to walk into. I would be the last to enter out of my friends and instantly lock eyes with Alex out there dancing on the dance floor wanting for me to join. In reality, she wasn't even in there and I was just waiting in this slow-moving snail pace of a line to get in.

Everyone kept on saying the line was moving quickly but to me, it felt like the line at Bizarro. David was almost finished with his American Spirit by the time we got close to the front. All I could think about was the dance floor inside. What is a dance floor like? What is a bar like? I could hear the bouncer's voice getting louder and louder as we approached the front. "Next…. Next… Next"

The reality of the situation was starting to set in and I could feel my heart beating faster and faster inside my chest as I got closer and closer to the front. I never thought I would truly be sneaking into a bar. There was going to be a shit ton of people older than me in there. I was hoping to just blend in. Most were significantly older than me, and half of them being girls, was giving me anxiety and already making me speechless as I walked towards the bouncer.

Before I could even collect my thoughts I heard the bouncer scream in front of me, "Next" and could feel his eyes piercing me. I was last in line for some reason; Steven and Matt were already on the other side of the line, inside the bar, waiting for me. I feel like it would have made more sense for me to go first and see if the fake ID trick actually got me inside before everyone else who had a valid ID but that's besides the fact now. The bouncer glanced at both Matt and Steven's ID and let them head in without even hesitating.

He grabbed my ID, looked it over longer than he did both of theirs. On the surface, I was doing my best to keep a stoic face. But on the inside, under my jeans, I was sweating, my knees were shaking, and I wanted to go home. I heard the little voice inside my head screaming at me in fear, reminding me of all the repercussions if I got caught, yelling at me to just run away. But I couldn't. I had to keep it cool to keep the night on. I kept my eye contact with the bouncer, stood on my tippy toes to look a little taller, and stood there strongly waiting for him to give me my brother's ID back.

After examining my ID for almost forty-five seconds, or I should say David's ID, he finally gave it back to me and let me in without saying a word. He just nodded his head for me to head inside to the bar. I heard him scream, "Next" again as I walked up to my brother inside to slip his ID back and followed the guys into the bar.

I did it! This was the first time in my life I have ever set foot in a bar and it was exhilarating. Just as the hotel confirmed everything I thought about college, the bar was everything I had envisioned it to be like. I mean I figured it was going to be wild in there, but what I walked into was lawless. Guys were pushing past girls, squeezing into whatever crevasse they could find to get to the front of the bar. Then there were some girls who would use their beauty and flirt their way through the crowds to get some free drinks from the sucker at the front of the bar.

The entire scene felt like it was a part of a movie. The first thing I needed to do now that I was inside was to find the bathroom. I haven't pissed since I've seen Alex in the woods and my bladder was about ready to explode like a volcano. Bar lesson 101: the men's bathroom at a bar is one of the most disgusting places on earth.

The entire bathroom felt gross to walk in. It very easily could've been water all over the floor that night but judging by the character of people in the bar, it was safe to assume that the floor was completely covered in piss. The one toilet in the bathroom was stuffed like a pepper with toilet paper. These people were savages.

I went right to the urinal, walking on my tippy toes the whole time, to take care of business and get out of there. As I was peeing I could hear a couple guys talking as they walked in and went straight into the clogged stall next to me talking about the girls they were with. They were having guys talk, gossiping about how attractive these girls they were with. Then the conversation paused for a moment and I heard a loud, "SNIFFFFF" from them.

I kept to myself, finished my business, and got out of the bathroom before they finished their business. The hand dryer was blowing out the last bit of air I needed to dry my hands right as they kicked open the door of their stall. Three dudes were all funneled out at the same time, not even trying to be discreet about what they were just doing. Each of them simultaneously wiped their nose, sniffing a few times only to wipe their nose again, refusing to blow their nose clear before they headed back out to the bar without even washing their hands.

A guy came in after them and I snuck out without even having to touch that filthy door they just got their paws all over. I pushed my way through the bathroom line that crowded the hallway. The bathroom line was the only place that had any sort of real system. They had all the guys on one side waiting for the bathroom while all the girls were waiting on the other side for theirs in a good ol' fashioned line- one thing the bar did not have.

The bathroom was my crash course introduction to the bar life. I didn't think I was short in any way but most of the guys that filled that bar were grown men. There weren't many of them that were under six feet tall. I couldn't see anything past them and had no idea where the hell my friends were standing. It was the first time I couldn't see over the crowd. Feeling short like this made finding my friends that much more laborious.

There were people everywhere. The bathroom line filled the hallway, the bar was jam-packed, and I think it was harder to move around inside the bar than it was at the tailgate. I said fuck it and pushed my way through the crowd hoping that I'd eventually crash into my friends. I had no sense of direction. I couldn't tell if I was heading towards the back of the bar or towards the front. All I knew was that I was walking away from the bathroom.

All of sudden I heard a familiar voice, "Yo Yo." It was my brother yelling through the crowd. I surveyed the space searching for his head to be above everyone else's. Perks of him being so tall. Once located him I headed straight toward them.

"Geez! Is it always like this in a bar because this is kind of an intimidating scene. I couldn't find you guys at all. I was starting to get a little worried." This was my first bar experience and it was a lot for me to take in.

They all shared a giggle, laughing at my ignorance. "It's like this everywhere; it sucks trying to order drinks." Steven made me feel a little less crazy for thinking this whole scene was obnoxious but it didn't change the fact of how much my heart was racing. I was beyond lucky; they had a beer waiting for me when I got back and I didn't have to fight my way to order one at the bar.

13

When we all finally had a drink in our hands we all found our happy place in unison. All of the tv's were playing the games Steven and my brother were betting on. It was gibberish to me whatever they were talking about. I had no idea what a push was, isn't a money line a Vegas term? What the hell is a unit? I couldn't understand a thing they were saying. Neither could Matt. So, he and I sat at the table with all the tv screens behind us, catching up on what college life was like while I did my best to explain to him the joys of the real world.

I asked him if we had any plans for the rest of the day, since all the plans seemed to flow through him. I came here with no plans, I didn't even have a place to sleep yet, all I came here to do was to hang out with my brother, Matt, and Steven, and now Alex, having the time of our lives.

Apparently there were no set plans for the night. It all depends on what a few people say about their houses, but we do at least have options.

Between Matt and my brother, who is freshly out of school there, I was certain we would be able to find something to get into that night.

My brother said his friends were going back to the hotel to keep partying before they got food from the restaurant near them. Matt's friends were just taking it slow until the night fell before they got after it. It was just the four of us right now and that was all we cared about.

Finally Matt, who was the man with the plan, asked David and Steven, "What's your guys' plan for the rest of the day?"

David answered, considering Steven and I were just here for the ride. "I think I'm going to go back and order some food with my old roommates. Then I was planning on coming out with you guys."

"I think I'm going to go with him for a little while. I haven't seen any of those guys in a while. I'll be back by the time you guys are ready to go out." Steven nodded his head towards as he was talking to us just so it was clear who he was talking about.

Matt turned to me and spoke for the both of us when he told them our plan, "We're gonna go to the cafe for a little bit then head back to the dorms. Just give me a call when you guys are ready to leave."

"That works for me, and just to be clear Matt, I don't want to step on any toes, is it alright if I come to the food hall with you guys?" I hate intruding on people's plans. I don't ever want to be a bother to anyone.

"Of course you are. By all means I want you to come with me and meet everyone." He would never have any issue with me tagging along.

"Matt, I'll give you a call when we're done and we'll regroup and see if you guys need anything," Steven said to Matt just before our group of four split into two groups of two.

"Okay cool, we'll probably need some booze by that time, but we'll figure it out later. We'll probably be pregaming in our dorms around then." We split into two different teams. It was my brother and Matt's brother going back to the hotel, while us younger folk hiked our way to this mecca of a food hall I've heard people talking about all day long. .

I desperately needed food. At this point in the day I may even need it more than I need to see

Alex. My stomach has been wailing and growling at me for damn near three hours now and it was beyond time I acknowledged it. All day long I've put my stomach on the back burner. Alex was all I was thinking about. I know I said I was going to enjoy the moments as they came earlier, but I was being pretentious. All I wanted to do was enjoy these moments with Alex... after I got food in my system.

"You guys wanna get going after this drive, this game's pretty much over. We might as well beat the rush at the bar to close out." David again proved to us that this wasn't his first rodeo. It was situations like this where we appreciated his experience and proudly followed him all morning long. This was his element, he had spent the last five years here. It has become his second home. If there was anyone I was going to follow blindly around Zoomass it was going to be my brother.

As one could have presumed, I was the last one out of all of us to finish my beer. I sipped my last sip while everyone was staring at me waiting to finish. I placed my beer on the table we were standing around and immediately my brother headed for the door. Everyone followed. "Oh, I'm sorry, were you guys waiting on me?"

I raced ahead to catch up with the group before we made it outside. On our way out we passed by the same bouncer still working at the front door and all said our goodbyes to him out of respect for letting us in. I don't think he knew how big that was for me. My brother was the first one out the door, followed by Matt, then Steven, then me, each of us saying goodbye and thank you.

As I was walking out the door the bouncer recognized us. We made eye contact as I was walking out the door and before I could get away I heard him call out to me, "Aye." We weren't getting out that easy. I think we all knew that there wasn't anything he could say to us, I mean we already paid our tabs, so there wasn't any trouble we could possibly be getting into.

Once he saw that he had all our attention he quietly eyed us up and down. And by us I mean my brother and I who were standing on opposite ends of our group. "Listen guys, I knew you guys shared IDs so he could get in. I was supposed to take it from you guys but when I saw all of you guys have similar last names and all looking alike, I figured it was some sort of family outing. You all look alike honestly. Out of respect I couldn't ruin your guys day. All I'm saying is just be careful using that ID, there's no way this dude is 6' 4"."

The bouncer pointed at me and I took that as my queue to leave.

"Wait, you knew it was mine the whole time?" David thought his plan was flawless. He couldn't believe that the guy knew the game we were playing. None of us could.

"Oh I knew immediately. I'm a big guy myself so naturally the first thing I look at on a guy's ID is their height and then I ask myself, 'Can I take them?' I knew this dude wasn't pushing six feet." The bouncer looked at me while he finished his statement so there was no discrepancy about who he was talking about.

What do you say to that? There we were thinking the entire time we were slick and pulled a fast one on the bouncer. Meanwhile he knew what we were doing the entire time. I guess at the end of the day he did let us all in after all knowing damn well I used my brother's ID. Finally, a couple words fell out of my mouth, "Thank you man, I appreciate you not getting me in trouble."

"Ah man, you're all good. Like I said I could tell you guys were all out together and it was too early to ruin your guys day." This had to be the nicest bouncer in the world. Yeah, so what if he's the first bouncer I met, but there's no way I'll meet anyone cooler than him. He hooked me up at that bar, letting me drink illegally so I could spend the day with my brothers. He was the real MVP of the day that day.

He could have drastically ruined our day, but he gave us the benefit of the doubt and gave us all a little hop in our steps. Things were going our way and there was this feeling in the air none of us could ignore- we were going to have a blast that night.

14

Together we kept walking back to the dorms, stumbling upon the same intersection where we met the cops before. They were still sitting on their horses' backs only letting us go certain ways. Matt and I were going to go back to the food hall to stuff our faces with some food while David and Steven went to the hotel to link up with their friends.

"Alright, I'm going to get us a ride. You guys are good, right?" I was David's responsibility that weekend and now that we were going separate ways I was on my own. I said we were good, gave him the nod, and he knew he didn't have to worry about me. We both could finally let loose for a while with people our own age, our own friends, without being judged by your brother..

"Alright, we'll give you a call when we're back at the dorms and gonna start pregaming." I wasn't David's problem anymore. Matt inherited me and took me under his wing. I was one step behind him following him like his shadow back to his dorm so he could change. I took this time for the walk to smoke my one hitter and get my mind right for the rest of the night.

He was adamant about not wearing the same clothes he had on at the tailgate out that night. He wanted to get home and change before he even thought about what was going on that night. I on the other hand had no issue with it. Mostly because my clothes were in my brother's car back at the hotel. I couldn't change even if I wanted to. If I went back to the hotel to get my clothes, there was no way I would find my way back to Matt's dorm. I figured I'd be alright wearing the same clothes.

It took us about fifteen minutes to get from wherever the bar was to where his dorm was. While we were climbing the stairs to his fourth-floor room, (apparently at the Zoo you would be shunned in the elevator if you made it stop on any floor earlier than the fifth. I assume it was because there were twenty-four floors so it honestly was just a nuisance to stop on ones people can walk to.) he told me that his roommate was there too and was coming out with us that night.

I instantly started smiling, "Drew's around tonight, hell yeah." I've only met him once before but we hit it off. We tore it up that night. He laughed at my stupid jokes so naturally he was cool in my books. I was excited to go out with him again. As soon as Matt opened his door there he was to greet us with a smile. It's going to be a good night.

"What's up guys, Tyler, how you've been?" He got up from his bed and we gave each other a bro hug. "It's been a while man." Evidently we left some memorable impressions on each other. He was just as eager to get after it tonight with me rolling in their clan as I was. Turns out he was two lanes over from us at the tailgate. We were just far enough not to run into each other.

We've all been drinking all morning and well into the afternoon, it was well beyond time for us to give our bodies a fighting chance against all this Devil's juice and get some solid food in our system. Once Matt slipped on his fresh new shirt he asked us, "Are you guys ready to go to the food hall?" Drew and I, who were already dressed and ready to go for the night, looked at him like he was crazy for asking us if we were ready.

"We're waiting on you, man." I couldn't let him put the blame on us. We shared a laugh together and left the dorms for the cafeteria or as they refer to it at the Zoo, McKinley. I've never been to college, seeing their dorms a moment ago was only the second time I've been inside any building affiliated with a college. I could not imagine what a cafeteria looked like. Especially after the tailgate.

I realized quickly that this was not a cafeteria by any means. It was like this massive food court you find at the mall just instead of filling your stomach with shitty mall food and msg, it's bigger and you're actually getting a full all you can eat meal ranging from sushi to chicken fingers to pancakes. Some real healthy meals for kids that live on their own at school. They're eating better than me.

The anxiety I had walking into the tailgate was nothing compared to the way McKinley caused my knees to shake. The entire scene was full of people running around racing to get food, spilling their drinks all over the floor, so they can hurry up and eat so they go up for seconds.

I knew why it was called the Zoo. It was pure anarchy in the cafeteria that day. People were drunk spilling their trays and drinks everywhere, others were hammered and couldn't even feed themselves. The poor sober people in there eating wanted nothing more than to get their food and get the hell out of there. They wanted no part of what was going on in the cafeteria that day and honestly, I don't blame them. I kind of wanted to run away with them.

Matt, as he was all day, was looking out for me. He showed me around all the different food stations they had and helped me pick my food. I filled my plate with the classic chicken fingers, fries, some turkey and mashed potatoes, with a second small plate full of mac and cheese avoiding crashing into everyone walking aimlessly. With his help and patience, I made it through the volatile food lines consisting of a bunch of hangry massholes without spilling a thing when I got to the table where his friends were sitting.

Truthfully though, I didn't feel any safer at the tables. It was treacherous just to get over there. We had to push past people just like we were at the tailgate to get to the table where all of his friends were sitting. Everyone there was smiling, laughing, and stuffing their faces with good vibes and food preparing themselves for the night. Once I sat down at the table I felt safe around them. I felt a little safer. After Matt introduced me to everyone and met the people I didn't know, I felt like I was a part of their group now.

There was something about the vibe in the cafeteria that was throwing me off. It could have only been me that felt it but I had this crazy hunch that we were on the verge of a food fight. You could feel it in the air; no adult supervision, people heavily intoxicated, and they all have their adrenaline running high. We had all the ingredients needed for a disaster. I was petrified and had to do my best to tame my nerves on the surface.

I did my best to ignore that hunch I had and enjoyed my time with new friends for dinner hoping I wouldn't have to hide for cover under the table. If there was going to be a food fight I like to think I would be safe. I mean there were like twenty of us. There's strength in numbers. We were the only group in the entire McKinley that pushed three tables together so everyone could fit. I knew I was safe with them knowing that no fool would dare to mess with this many of us.

I loved being around them. They were yelling over each other trying to talk to everyone, busting each other's balls, it made me feel like home. Like I was at Sunday Dinner back at my Grammys when we would all pack her house to stuff our faces together just like we are now.

Their group of friends was close. One of the closest groups of friends I've ever met. A group of friends I admired. They all came there and found something in each other that worked. They all hang out all the time, they always want to be around one another. They were a group of friends that everyone epitomized and I just happened to be lucky enough to be a part of it. Even if it is only for a night.

The lingering feeling of a food fight vanished from my mind and I got lost in a good time. We finally gave our bodies enough nutrients to battle against the alcohol so we could keep on going all night long. I wasn't stressed about getting hit in the face with mac and cheese anymore. Instead, I was overcome with tears of joy laughing at the stories they had to tell about the Zoo.

15

I couldn't tell you how long we were in Mckinley for. I tend to eat rather quickly and felt like I was just waiting forever for everyone else to finish their food so they could figure out the next move. I thought it was the perfect opportunity for me to get some fresh air and smoke my dugout while they made plans for the night. And I wanted to get out of there just in case I was right about that whole food fight thing. I did not want to be a part of it.

At this point it's been a while since I've had a drink in my hand or have smoked. I needed a little something like that to get ready to restart the night. It was a Saturday, the sun was starting to set and I did not want to start sobering up now. If I had any chance of being able to come up with anything smooth to say to Alex I knew I needed some liquid courage to find it. Or at least a couple hits do the same thing.

I was around the corner of the entrance to the cafeteria thinking to myself how contrasting my life would be if I had gone to college. I was just watching all the kids still walking around with backpacks and books clearly still having some work to do on a Saturday while others were barely able to stand up on their own two feet too drunk to go on for the rest of the night. I wondered what crowd I would have gotten lost in. Then ultimately I came to the conclusion that it was a good idea I didn't go to college.

Matt and Drew found me around the corner and shook me from my daze, "Do you want to come back to the dorm with us? Everyone was planning on coming back to our place and pregaming after they got ready and stuff before we went out." Matt was asking me nicely but it was more of a rhetorical question. I was his guest and truthfully wouldn't know what to do if he wasn't here for me.

I smiled and sarcastically said, "I don't really have many options, do I?"

We all laughed and Matt brought us back, "Come on let's start heading back that way now. I got some booze there we can start with when we get there." That was all I needed to hear to get some pep in my step and follow them back through campus. Apparently back the same way we came. I had no sense of direction.

We were in the middle of their campus and felt like this was probably the closest I will ever be to a college student... and it's a freaking Saturday. A homecoming nonetheless. It was just the sheer fact of being in Umass all day long like this, eating in the cafeteria made me feel like I went there. I was completely engulfed in the college atmosphere that it was starting to feel like I was a part of it.

There I was on a Saturday, spending the entire day and I'm sure we'll party well into the next morning uncovering this school for what it truly is. The types of people I saw walking through campus were eclectic. Never again will I ever be around so many people in such a small radius than like when you're at the Zoo. It was wild to me how drastically different their worlds were living at school than mine was out in the real world.

In the real world I'm hoping to find that special someone to always have around. It's how my family was raised, we're all lovers. It's just different if my heart isn't beating for someone else. Alex has been that special someone whose heart beats with mine. Someone I want to see, if I can spend forever with.

Which is exactly why I'm glad I never went to college. If I didn't have anyone to give all of my love to then I would be finding a way to give someone my love. There's no telling where I'd be or what I would have found myself lost in if I had gone to college. Maybe if I went to college I would have graduated college with a couple of kids, three STDs, and some liberal arts degree. Not exactly how you plan things to go. I think these overnight weekend trips are more than enough for me.

I wasn't out there that night to just find someone to give my love to or to take me back to their dorm so I had a place to sleep. I came there to see my friends, and now with the obvious developing situation, I'm hoping to finally connect with Alex. She's someone I have seriously been crushing on and this was my night to seize the moment. While we were walking back to the dorms I had to ask again, "Have you heard anything from Alex?"

"I haven't heard anything from her but I also haven't texted her either. I was going to check in with her when we were on our way out." The man with a plan, my tour guide, was making everything happen tonight. "I'll make sure we'll cross paths with her tonight, don't worry." Matt is a true best friend. One I've been beyond lucky to have met and even luckier to call him my best friend.

"Wait, Tyler, do you have a crush on Alex or are you just trying to hook up with her?" Drew chimed seeing my face turn beat red, impossible for me to deny the truth.

"I guess you could call it a crush. I've had a crush on her for years now, we've just never been able to act on it. I'm hoping tonight that we can connect for a little more than just staring at each other from across the room. It'll be the first time both of us have been single at the same time. I just need a chance to talk to her before someone else does." Drew clearly already could tell there was something going on between her and me so I figured I'd fill him in and have him in my corner hyping me up all night.

Before we went inside we all took an extra second outside of their dorm to each take another hit from my one hitter before we went inside to start our night. When we opened the door to enter the dorm there was a lady sitting at a desk in the lobby waiting for us. A desk that was vacant the last time we came to his dorm. One I didn't think twice about. The lady seemed to be our age but wasn't on the same wavelength we were on. She immediately made her presence felt, bombarding us with a million questions. "What are you guys doing here? Do you live here?"

"Yeah, we're up on the sixth floor." Matt answered without any hesitation.

"All of you guys?" She was skeptical of us.

"Yeah we're roommates and he lives down the hall." Matt was handling her questions calmly. I on the other hand had no idea who the hell we were answering to. Who was she to come at us like this?

"Alright just go in, I don't have the scanner set up yet." She didn't seem happy about just letting us walk by but we never hesitated. We headed straight to the stairs and out of her sight. On our ascent to their dorm they informed me that she was RA and it honestly sounded like a boring way to spend your time at college. What I gathered about their job is that essentially they're like the no-fun police. Am I wrong?

Apparently they have this strict rule that each person is only allowed two guests. Which meant between the two of them, we were only allowed four guests at a time in their dorm. If my math was right, counting people at dinner and adding my brother and Steven, we were well past their four-person limit. There had to be at least twelve of us that were all supposed to be meeting here. I didn't say anything to them but mathematically things didn't add up.

I assumed they had a plan. "That was awesome she didn't ask to see our student IDs." Drew was talking to Matt because I had no idea what he was saying.

"I was just thinking that we'll have to figure out a way to get everyone in here." I'm just glad they're aware of the obstacle that's in front of us.

16

It was just the three of us to start. It was clear to me they have had people over their dorm before. Matt connected to the speaker, Drew brought out the booze, and the three of us started our night together while everyone else went home to nap or get ready.

Of course Matt started the night with Chance, blasting him through the speaker. When the beat came in it lifted me off of the bean bag to my feet and I started dancing along to the music. The three of us were jamming out, manifesting some good vibes for us for the rest of the night.

As Matt was on his phone setting up a queue of bangers, the music was interrupted by his text notification, and he sighed in excitement and said, "Guys, guess who just texted me?" He looked at me, then looked over at Drew, then back over at me disappointed neither of us even had a guess. I shrugged my shoulders and looked over at Drew assuming Matt was asking him rather than me.

Matt didn't let our lack of guesses or participation ruin his vibe. Deservingly so, he took time to answer his text before he told us who he was talking about. After he sent his text he took his breath and opened his mouth to speak just as his music was interrupted again by another message.

"Could you turn off your notifications Matt?" I was curious, I wanted to know who was texting him but we had a more pressing issue. Nothing irks me more than the music being interrupted by text message after text message after text message.

Matt just looked at me and grinned, "It's Alex."

My heart skipped a beat. I had to control my feelings. I didn't care that she was the one interrupting the music. This was what I had been waiting for all day long. This was it, this was my chance to see her tonight and see if we can finally connect together the way I know we can. I had to keep my composure. All I heard was her name, I couldn't get too worked up yet I didn't even know what she said. I took a deep breath before I let my mouth say anything, "What did she say?"

Matt opened up his phone and read off her message to us, "She said she was going back to her place to get ready now and then was heading over to her friends' house to pregame before they went out. But she said she wants to meet up with us tonight for sure." I couldn't hold it anymore. I started smiling like I was back in middle school and found out my crush liked me too. She said she wanted to hang out with all of us but me having the narcissistic ego I do, told myself that she only wanted to see me. I convinced myself that she wanted to see me as much as I wanted to see her.

My smile was the only tell that I was excited to see her. I was fighting to keep it all on the inside. On the inside there were fireworks shooting off, my heart was exploding with love, and all I wanted to do was express it to the world. I thought I was keeping it cool but keeping it cool was the last thing I was doing. I mean this was the news I've been waiting to hear all day long. How could I contain myself? I needed to take a moment to myself to process everything, "Oh really, is she!? Hell yeah, that's awesome. Hey, where's your bathroom in this dorm?" I didn't even wait to hear an answer, I just needed a second for myself.

"Oh, we actually have one on our floor. Go down the hallway and the guys room is going to be on the right." Drew was quick to answer. The butterflies and excitement were slowly turning to nerves and anxiousness. I speed-walked to the bathroom and splashed some water on my face to get my composure. It's finally here. A moment of her and I together and finally able to connect without any restrictions. No boyfriends, no girlfriends, just us. I looked at myself in the mirror one last time and told myself that tonight's the night and walked back to their dorm smiling like a kid in a candy store with some newfound confidence.

When I got back Matt had just finished prepping some more mixies for us to keep the night rolling. I was handed one of them as soon as I walked in. While he handed me the mixie he told me, "Some of my friends are coming by in a sec. They live a couple floors upstairs so they won't be long." After some more quick math and it looks like that would be another couple of guest passes we'll have freed up for people to snake some more people in.

Sure enough a moment later, we heard their knock on the door. It was their three buddies with their hands full of handles of vodka and racks of beer. (Our rack of beer is a thirty pack) I recognized two of his friends from earlier at the tailgate and was introduced to this third dude. Matt poured them some mixies while they each shotgunned a beer and our Saturday night was off with a bang.

17

We had a couple rounds of mixies arguing about sports and girls with just us guys until Matt's music was interrupted by a phone call from his brother. He stepped away to talk to him while the rest of us kept on arguing about how the Patriots would win the Super Bowl that year.

Matt was in the background only saying words like, "yeah" and "okay" agreeing with whatever the plan was. When he hung up the phone we all went silent, curious what the move was.

"David and Steven are coming this way to pregame with us. They're bringing Nick too." That damn near solidified it for me. When I heard Nick was coming I knew this night was going to be one to remember. Nick was our brother's friend but tonight he was all of our friends. Nick is the type of guy that can start a party at a funeral.

I actually kind of felt cool knowing we were accumulating this massive crew together mixed with current Zoomass students, former

Zoomass students, and friends who are here visiting to go out together. We had a squad, we had booze, it was everything we needed for a legend wait for it… dary night.

"Hey, do you guys mind coming down with me so we can sign them in." Matt asked Drew and Scott, who lived upstairs, to follow him downstairs so they could scan them in. I could see the math working out now. They were inviting more people that lived in the building so they had plenty of swipes to get the whole tailgate in here. I wasn't worried about the swipes anymore.

As soon as they left and the door closed I could feel the juices flowing. There was no doubt in my mind that tonight was going to be epic. It was maybe fifteen seconds later Matt kicked open the door with our brothers and Nick following behind. "Damn that was quick, you guys went down and back already." One of Matt's friends beat me to the question.

"Hell no, we didn't have to check in. I used to live here, this was my building. I had to check the RA and make sure she was doing her job right. We're all good." Nick came in hot, as he always does. He always brings the energy everywhere he goes and it's contagious. We all felt it instantly when he walked into the room. They all took a second to introduce themselves to everyone as Matt filled their hands with mixies, and we turned the night back on.

Matt finally silenced his phone and had the music blasting without any interruptions. It was a Saturday night at the Zoo and we were ready to take on the night. There was no such thing as a noise complaint on a Saturday night. The entire dorm was partying, there was no one who would have called a noise complaint.

With Nick leading the way, busting the first move, he got all of us forming a dance circle around the room. Each one of us took turns getting down and grooving to the music. I was standing in front of the door when someone pushed it open and hit me in my back. It was more of Matt's friends funneling in.

They had said they knocked but with the music blasting and the dance floor being so hot, none of us could hear their knock. I was right on the other side of the door and couldn't even hear it. I could only get hit by it.

They went around and said their hellos and when they finished, we turned the music back on. Looking around the room, seeing how full our dance floor was, I realized we were well over the two person guest limit. There had to be already about fifteen of us in the dorm.

Initially it was just his friends that lived on the floor. Then the girls that were living on the floor below him came up, then all of a sudden we had a full blown party going on in his dorm. We had music blasting, drinks flowing, and everyone up in the dance circle getting their turns to get down.

Standing in front of the door again, not learning my lesson, I'm hit in the back with the door for a third time. This time it was a group of girls that didn't even apologize for hitting me. They were those "mean girl" types of girls. I didn't know them and as attractive as I thought they were, I had no urge to get to know them. They didn't even apologize for slamming the door into my back.

Nor did I care about any girls. In my eyes, all I cared about was Alex. I kept on reminding myself that tonight is the night we finally get our chance together. I wasn't going to blow my chance with her just to impress my friends and have fun with someone for one night. It wasn't worth it to me. I kept on hoping that the next person that hit me with the door was her.

Until I saw her I was going to make the most of the night. I met Nick out in the middle of the dance circle. Nick is known around our town as one of the best dancers. Every party there was, anywhere we were, he would always find a way to dance, and he was dope at it. It didn't even matter if there wasn't any music. He would find a speaker or blast his phone, move some furniture out of the way, and dance all night long. Just as he did in Matt's dorm.

My dance moves on the other hand were appalling. I have zero rhythm. I couldn't stay on beat with a song even if my life depended on it. Which is typically why I don't dance but that night, being surrounded by friends, and our good vibes radiating from one another, I couldn't fight the urge to get out there and dance.

I won't lie to you, the only reason I got out there was because I had a little liquid courage running through my veins. All it took was a couple of whatever Matt was making and I was ready. Nick met me in the center circle and started things off. He could do this thing with his arms, waving them perfectly in rhythm with the song, twisting his body in ways I never could. His pockets were full of dance moves that were far deeper than mine.

Then when he finished, he stretched his arm out to me pointing as if he was saying, "your turn" and concluded his beat down. Truthfully I didn't want to go in after him. I would have much rather have gone first so I didn't make a fool of myself going after him and then letting him embarrass me. I was content with that, but having to go after him is a completely different game.

All that confidence I had was fading away the more I thought about it. I couldn't think. I let the Devil's Juice do its thing and reacted to the music. I had a few sly moves up my sleeve and it was time for me to let them loose.

I came into the center of the dance floor firing. I pushed my make-believe shopping cart right out to the center, stopping to grab items on the shelf, filling up my cart, immediately setting the tone. I shoved my imaginary shopping cart over to Nick, replacing it with some imaginary q tips, proceeding to clean one ear then the other with the beat of the music.

That was my whole pocket full of dance moves. Hence why I wanted to go first, but based on everyone's reaction and judging by Nick's face it felt like I won. At least initially I thought, but I neglected how competitive he was. He sprung back into the circle the second I stepped out. Again he was out there jumping around, spinning on the floor, pretending to throw things up and catch them, all perfectly on beat. I didn't stand a chance.

At this point, after being on the verge of victory, I wasn't going to go down without a fight. I stepped back up to him in the center of the dance floor and battled. I started off with some random moves, waving my hands and popping my chest along with the music but when I broke out the "You can't see me" from John Cena I got the crowd right back in my corner. Everybody was screaming at the top of their lungs dumbfounded by my moves.

Nick started stepping towards me dancing, so I danced my way to the center of the dance floor to meet him. Him and I could dance all night. We danced until the song ended knowing that we were going to be dancing later. This was still only the pregame, we needed to conserve our energy for the rest of the night. I mean I still had no idea what the plan was for the night but I sure hope we find ourselves at a place with a dance floor. I, by no means, was ready to quit dancing.

I left the dance floor and headed to make another drink. David and Steven were hanging over by the beer talking while I interrupted their conversation to praise Nick, "Damn man, he's a wicked good dancer. In no way can I keep up with him."

Steven nodded at me laughing while looking over at Nick, "Look at him, he's still going. He loves dancing. You should have seen him at the wedding last month. He looked like Leo in The Great Gatsby."

"Back when we were going to school here together, that was how I was able to find him at parties. When it was time to go I would just go searching for the dance floor and find him there. It actually made it wicked easy for me to find him." David spent most of his time partying with Nick while they were here. It makes sense to me now why he's become so proficient at dancing; he's had the damn practice for it.

18

While I was pouring myself another drink Matt was next to me answering all the texts he's been ignoring for the past hour. "What's up man, how you doing?" I haven't talked to him since the dance floor started.

"I think we're late." That was all he said to me before he stopped the music to get everyone's attention. "Guys, everyone is getting ready to head over to Carriage Lane now. We should start heading that way." He advised us all to grab our beers, top off our mixies, and down the road to get the party started.

We ran down those stairs like a stampede, eager for our night to officially start. The RA looked mortified watching us race out the door in front of her. Each of us had our hands full with sodas and beers for our walk. The only ones who had their hands free were me and the other smokers as we passed around a blizzy while trailing behind the rest of the group.

When we finished smoking I sped up from the back of the herd to catch up with Matt and get a sense for whatever the hell we were doing that night, "I'm not sure yet honestly. I think a bunch of people are coming out this way. We just don't know where we are partying yet. This street is full of kids who go to school here. It's close enough we can walk to it from campus but it's just far enough away that it's off campus so they have to follow our stupid rules."

David, who was in the middle of the group, heard us talking and chimed in, "Last time I was here there was a party at every single house on the street. My buddies and I just hopped around all night going from house to house. It got so out of control that the whole street had to run from the cops. I ripped my favorite pair of jeans that night trying to hop a fence." I couldn't wait to see what Carriage Lane had to offer. I had no idea what to expect. All day long I keep on learning new reasons as to why they called it Zoomass. I feel like tonight being on this infamous street, we will solidify it. I just kept hoping that I would see the one person who would make this night perfect.

As we approached the street I could hear the voices from people echoing through the streets. The closer and closer we got the more and more it started to sound exactly like the tailgate earlier. When we turned onto Carriage Lane it felt like deja vu. There were just as many people on the street as there were people at the tailgate. It felt like the entire school was partying together that day. I honestly thought there was a block party going on the way we filled the streets. Nope, it was just another Saturday on Carriage Lane.

Most of us that were out right now were underclassmen. I guess "we" typically just hang out on the streets waiting for someone's house to open up. If these were only the underclassmen then once the rest of the people come, it will only be a matter of time until the cops do. It will be another night of running from the cops.

I guess that's typically how things go around there. From what I could tell it looked like only a couple of houses were having parties right now and we needed to find the one that would let all twenty of us come in. David moved to the front of our group to lead us to a place to drop our drinks and party. I followed him to the front being his shadow, wanting to help in every way I could to find a place to drink. We took it upon ourselves to find the perfect spot for all of us to party that night.

Between the group of us, we had enough alcohol and drugs to supply a whole party with everything they needed to party. We just needed someone to let us in. The first house we saw on the corner of the street had strobe lights flashing through their windows and was the only house this early with a line around the corner with people waiting to get in from the front door. Following my brother's lead our entire group flowed like a school of fish to the back of the house.

David knew that if we came in through the back door security would be weaker if not non-existent. Turns out there was only one little kid, and coming from me (who has had the same baby peach fuzz and all since the day I was born) knew that we were both too young to be at a place like this, guarding the door. David, being the older brother, knew this was our chance to sneak in.

He and I approached the lone kid at the back door while the rest of our army waited in the yard for our okay. He was undoubtedly intimated with us before we even got to the door. I mean I know I sure as hell would have shit my pants if I saw that many people coming towards me being led by my six-four brother. David didn't even drop his beers before he walked to the kid and asked him straight up, "Hey man, can we come inside?"

"Sorry guys…" The kid was nervous, we could hear it from his tone of voice, "You have to go in through the front to get in, I'm sorry.." He apologized twice. His voice even cracked a little at the end there. If we were going to wait in line to get into this house we had to know it was worth it.

David was curious whose house this was that was bumping the way it was. He knew this street had a few of the sports teams' houses and was curious as to whose house this one belonged to. "Whose house is this anyway?"

"It's the swim team's." The kid looked embarrassed to say it out loud. His face turned red saying it out loud. There was no way we were going to be pushed around by a kid at the pool house.

My brother and I both had enough to drink that we weren't thinking about anything we said before we said it. If we thought it we said it, and I spoke the first thing that came to me. "Wait, this is the swim team's house." For a moment that night my brother and I's Masshole came out.

"Yeah." The kid could only look at the ground while he said it. He knew it sounded pathetic saying it out loud and wanted nothing to do with us.

I was only thinking about getting a laugh and didn't even consider his feelings when I yelled back to the army behind us, "Guys this is the swim team's house." I was mean to him, "Does anyone even want to go here?"

David asked the guy quietly before things escalated, "We really can't just come in for a little?"

"I can't, I'm sorry you have to go in the front." The guy wasn't being confrontational with us at all. He handled it exceptionally, he didn't deserve me roasting him like I did. I was just a dick to him for no reason at all.

"How bad did you have to mess up at a swim meet to get backdoor duty on a Saturday night? At the swim house nonetheless?" I was ruthless and an asshole. I wasn't saying these things to belittle him. I was only saying them because I thought it was funny. The swim team, of all places, I thought would have been the quietest place on the street. Nor did I think they would ever be wild enough to have to have security at every door. Honestly, I was just bitter that he didn't let us in. I was hoping to find that guy again later so I could apologize to him. We left before we said anything that crossed the line.

19

We had our fun with him and went our separate ways without completely ruining that kid's night. It was bad enough he was on back-door duty at the Swim house. He already had it bad, we didn't have to add to it. Like a pack of wolves we made our way down the street in search of another place to party. It didn't matter to us if it was the swim house or some sort of trap house, all we wanted to do was find a place for all of us to dance.

I had this feeling like we forgot something at the dorm and it didn't register to me until Steven mentioned it, "We should have brought your speaker for the walk." We had the people, had the alcohol, the only thing we were missing was Matt's speaker.

"I was just thinking that. It would be so perfect right now. I can't believe I forgot it." You could tell Matt was disappointed with himself. He wanted to be the best host possible and something as little as forgetting the speaker was a big deal.

"I'm sure we'll be able to blast the music once we find someone's house. If not I'll get some going." If anyone was going to find a speaker it was going to be Nick.

Carriage Lane was one of the straightest streets I had ever seen. For about half a mile it was perfectly straight. There weren't even any curves in the lines on the street, no hills, the street was as straight as an arrow. Part of the street was lit by the streetlights while the other part of the street was shining with a rainbow of flashing lights coming from all the houses on the street.

It was the first time I turned around to see the street since we left the Swim team's house. I was going to tell Steven something but lost all train of thought when I saw our group multiplied. We became this home for all the runaways of Umass looking for a place to party. We kept on picking up stragglers as we walked down the street. It got to the point where I knew less than half of the people that were in our group. The only thing I did know was that we were all looking for a good night.

David was still leading the charge. "This house has their lights on, let's check it out." I thought he was kidding. There's no way he's just going to knock on their door and ask them if they were having a party. But there he went walking up their path to their front door. He was my brother, I couldn't let him go alone and I followed right behind him with the rest of our crew behind us on the street.

David got to the door and knocked on the catchy jingle trying to see if anyone was home. No one answered. He knocked again with his same knock, and still no one answered. Instead of knocking for a third time he just reached for the doorknob to see if the house was open to check if anyone was home.

With one twist of the knob and a single push we were inside the house. He stepped inside and I was right behind him like his shadow into the foyer of the house. David yelled, "Hello?" wondering if anyone was actually home and there was no answer. He peeked his head into the living room, yelled again hello, and saw no one. I looked into the room on the left and it was only filled with boxes and this disgusting couch. It was covered in stains, the leather was ripped up, and it was not a couch anyone would sit on.

We were on our way to their kitchen to see if anyone was there cooking with their headphones on or something when we heard a voice shouting angrily from upstairs, "Hey what the hell are you guys doing in my house!?" My brother and I looked up the stairs of the foyer to see this hairless dude wearing nothing but his loose pair of boxer briefs, which I didn't know people wore after high school, looking down on us, revealing his boys from our vantage point. It's kind of hard to take someone seriously when you can see their half chub and their balls hanging lower than their underwear but we did our best.

My brother didn't flinch. While I stood there processing seeing a grown man naked like I was in a Planet Fitness locker room, played dumb and asked him, "Oh I'm sorry, I heard you guys were having a party tonight?"

"Does it look like we're having a party tonight?" The guy was clearly pissed at us. Rightfully so, I mean we did just kind of barged into his house. The shadows behind the guy started to move and I thought the place was haunted. A few seconds later it turns out it wasn't a ghost but this girl who found some of his clothes to put on came out reiterating, "We're not having a party."

The guy was on some sort of high horse talking down to us from upstairs and repeated himself like he had authority, "We're not having a party tonight."

Everyone else was still outside waiting for us to give them the okay to come inside. David and I looked at each other and agreed this wasn't our battle. We were wrong for welcoming ourselves into this guy's house uninvited. Clearly this dude was enjoying a night with his girlfriend and had more important things to do than party with us. We were just the assholes that ruined his night.

David apologized to the guy bullshitting him from above, "We must be at the wrong house I'm sorry. I guess I got the wrong house" and we started to leave his house. Right before he stepped outside David yelled back to the dude upstairs, "Well maybe next time you should lock the door when you're upstairs having fun with your girlfriend. You would have avoided this whole situation." They both were up there speechless. We walked out of there smiling cheek to cheek.

The group got silent while we were walking back to them. Everyone funneled towards wondering if we could get in. They wanted to know if we could party there. All eyes were on David. He cheered out with excitement, "They didn't want us. So, let's go on to the next one!"

For the third time that night we headed down Carriage Lane in search of a party. We saw a few houses that had lights on but we couldn't see anyone inside so walked right past them. We were just looking to have some fun that night, we weren't trying to catch any felonies. If we didn't see people inside we weren't going in.

20

I had no idea how this block party thing was going to turn out. From what I could tell, it seemed like everyone was just hanging out on the street in their own groups like it was some high school cafeteria. We all were waiting to see which house was going to be the one hosting the party. This weekend was an anomaly, even my brother couldn't believe we hadn't found a place to drop our beers yet.

David said to me as we led the way, "We have the golden ticket to get into any party; We have the booze, we have the girls, and are ready to tear it up." He told me about this one unwritten rule that exists in college; if you can sustain the golden ratio of having more girls and booze than guys, you'll be welcome into any party.

Third time a charm and David saw another house with the lights but this time he could see a bunch of guys sitting in their living room enjoying their Saturday night watching football games. He looked at me and I was already looking at him and again we heard the words neither one of us had to say out loud, "This was our spot."

David headed for the door, followed by me, then Steven, then Nick. We all stood at the door with our hands full of housewarming gifts as if it would be enough to get us inside. David knocked on the door with the same jingle he used at every other house. We could see a kid get up from the couch in the living room and come to the front door to open it for us. He didn't even have a chance to say anything to us. As soon as he opened the door Nick barreled himself inside and the rest of our group followed right behind him.

David yelled to the kid who opened the door for us, over all the stampede of people running into their house playing dumb again, "We heard you guys were having a party tonight. We came by to check it out."

"We were just having a chill guys' night. We're not having a party here tonight." The guy was trying to say no to us, he was even shaking his head no for us to see, but it was too late. Most of our group was already inside and once the other groups of people on the street saw us funneling in, they were right behind us. All of a sudden there were damn near sixty people that none of us knew filling this random guy's house.

He was yelling over the crowd back to David. I was standing right next to my brother and could hear this guy loud and clear. I don't know if my brother actually didn't hear him or chose not to but he yelled back to him, "Don't worry about it. We'll stay out here and man the door for you all night. Go enjoy the party, tonight's going to be a blast."

David spoke with such confidence I think that's why the kid turned around to go back inside and accepted that they were hosting a party tonight. Or maybe it was because we had already filled their house and there was still half a street full of people trying to come in. It's hard to stop it from happening now.

He proceeded right to the living room to tell his friends what was happening and I could see through the window the group was torn. Two of them started smiling and were excited for the party. While the other kids looked timid and overwhelmed by the abrupt rush of an insane amount of people in their house uninvited. I get how he feels, I'd be the same way if this was my place but fortunately it wasn't. And good for us the kids that were against the party were outvoted.

One of the guys quickly grabbed the last slice of pizza they had and then they all left the living room embracing the party. Even the guy who didn't want to party finally accepted it. This was it, they accepted us being here, and we finally found a place for us to drop our beers and tear up a dance floor.

I saw Nick walk right up to the guy who let us in through the window thanking him for their hospitality with one of his beers. He was making some small talk with the guy but I knew it was for one reason only and that was to find their speaker and connect to it so he could be the DJ for the rest of the night. There was nothing he loved more than being the man in control of the music.

In the span of maybe two minutes, these guys went from chilling on their couch to hosting the biggest party on the street. It was up to David and I to keep this party under control. We kept our word and stood as the bouncers for the party creating the vibe we wanted that night for everyone inside. For our friends' sake, we made sure to keep that two-to-one girl-to-guy ratio. We were going to create the best party this street has ever seen.

Even though I really didn't give two shits about any of the girls walking in, even if some of them are jaw-droppingly attractive, I kept on hoping that the next girl that decided to stroll into our party was going to be her. I haven't heard anything about Alex since it was just Matt, Drew, and I back before our night started. It was getting to the point where I was thinking I needed to start praying that we would cross paths tonight. I don't know how many nights I'd spend sleepless knowing that the one time we had a chance to connect together ended with us never even seeing one another.

If I never saw her then I at least wanted to ensure that all of our friends were having the time of their lives. I was completely content with spending the night with my brother as bouncers for this party. We were out there checking IDs, making people sing their favorite Justin Bieber songs just to get into the party we started. Hell, we were even profiting by getting some people to pay us cash to come into this guy's house.

Periodically the kids that were living in the house, or should I say the ones hosting the party, would come out to thank us for creating such an incredible party. It was like clockwork, each time one of them came back from getting another drink they would stop by us outside to thank us for setting this all up for them. Then they would promptly hand each of us a cold Bud Light as a reward for controlling the crowd. This night was turning into everything I thought it'd be.

21

Neither David or I ever set foot inside the guy's place. We took turns taking a piss around the corner in the bushes, but never left their door unattended. This was our party and we didn't want to let anyone in that was going to kill our vibe. We had friends inside taking shots, some were running the pong table, and the rest were occupying the dance floor and every single one of them was having the time of their lives.

The night was perfect. When I looked through the mirror it looked like everyone was cheesing with drinks in their hands surrounded by some of their best friends and all these new ones. No one could have asked for anything more. The night was perfect. There was only one thing that would make my night perfect and I kept my fingers crossed behind my back that I would see Alex walking up the front steps to this house. If and only when she walks up those stairs, then it would be officially deemed perfect.

David and I loved working the front door. Or at least I did. I'm an average-sized guy. If I'm wearing the right shoes I may be six feet tall. Otherwise I'm tiny and will always be overshadowed or physically looked down on. For me to be a bouncer that night was a big deal personally.

It was the first time I've ever felt any authority or even any sort of control over any situation. My brother, on the other hand, seemed like he'd done this a thousand times before. He's a much bigger guy than I was obviously, so he's naturally found himself in this role. He was on the other side of the door backing me up and I don't think I ever stood taller. I was able to tell people to go pound sand which I normally would avoid at a party. It was like I was finally able to compensate for my Napoleon complex.

"Hey Tyler!" I heard this comforting voice, one I recognized. One I know I heard earlier that day. I was instantly knocked off of my complex and came back down to reality. It was the voice I'd been craving to hear all day long. There she was, the next girl in line. She saw me before I saw her. She finally came out, "Can we come inside?"

I was frozen when I saw her. I pinched my leg just to confirm this was real and I wasn't that drunk, "Yes of course, you're welcome to come in." That was the smoothest line I could come up with... Pathetic I know. She was standing there with her friends and I was in awe. There she was standing in front of me asking me if she could come party with us.

I was cheesing cheek to cheek knowing that we finally have a night where we can be together. She brushed by me gently as she walked inside. Before she got lost in the crowd she stopped to look back at me to share one last moment together then disappeared inside.

She was styling at the tailgate. I didn't think she could look any better than she did. But there she was showing up at that house proving me wrong. I kept on thinking about her all day long and how attractive she was. I had no idea she was going to go back to her dorm and get better looking. She was so beautiful and she wasn't even trying.

She wasn't dressed provocatively like everyone else was at the party. She wasn't there to impress anyone, she was there to have a fun Saturday night with her friends. She came in with her style, rocking her black skinny jeans, vans, and a Nirvana t-shirt. Dressed exactly how I always pictured my future wife to be dressing.

I had to go in and talk to her but I didn't know what to say. My knees were shaking and my hands got clammy just a moment ago, I wasn't ready to talk to her. I wasn't even sure I'd be able to say anything to her. All day I was waiting for this moment you would think I would have had something to say.

"Are you gonna go inside and talk to her?" David shook me from my mind confused as to why I was still standing outside. He knew this was all I had been waiting for all day long.

"I'm going, give me a second. I don't know what to say." She went right to the foyer and walked into the living room where I could still see her through the windows. She found Matt and was saying hi to the rest of our friends. I could see her turning all the guys' heads as soon as she walked into the house. She was glowing when I saw her outside. I was the only one that could see her shining. Now she was there shining for everyone else to see, impossible for anyone to ignore.

She stole my heart a long time ago but at the tailgate, it was rejuvenated. Now seeing her out here tonight I've fallen even more in love with her than I ever thought I could love. The way she was smiling, the way she was setting off fireworks in my heart, I knew it was love. That real kind of love and I needed to talk to her.

"Go talk to her dude, you'll be fine. She's clearly into you. Have you noticed anyone else stopping outside to say hi to you before they go inside?" He made a valid point; aside from the people we made earn their spot inside, no one cared to even say hi. She was the only one.

"That's true, juuusssst give me a second.." I've had all day to figure out what to say to her right now. All day and I have nothing. I couldn't keep my head from running for a second to find anything to say. Knowing that this was our moment to either make or break us was giving me enough pressure to push me to the edge of a panic attack.

"Just go dude, you'll figure it out once you start talking." David was rooting for me.

My hands were sweating, I got this sudden stomach ache, and I was stuttering just talking to my brother. I had to make my move. "I'm actually wicked nervous." I felt better admitting out loud but it didn't erase the nerves I was feeling, but I knew it was time.

"Go find her, you'll be alright." He slapped me on the back and I turned around to head inside.

"Here goes nothing," I said to myself before I stepped foot into the party for the first time that night.

22

It was a drastically different vibe inside that house than what we were dealing with outside. We had the outside under control. No one was causing a scene because they knew they wouldn't get in. But inside was a different story. It was like once these people got inside it became total anarchy. People were using vases for their mixies, the pictures that were hanging in the house were now all upside down, and everyone was using their outside voices indoors. I had to play bumper cars again pushing through the living room looking for Alex.

I saw her through the window of the living room and figured that was the place to start. I was powerless inside. Outside people listened to me. In here, I have to fight through the crowd just like everyone. I walked through the living room and never saw her. I went to the next room, which was the kitchen, with my feet sticking to the soda that was spilt all over the floor with each step. You could tell it was a bunch of guys that lived there. The whole place looks like it hasn't been cleaned in months. My friends migrated to the kitchen but were without Alex.

"Matt, what's up man, how's your night going?" I asked, hoping that all David and my hard work had paid off inside and people were having a blast.

"Tyler, long time no see." He introduced me to his new friends and we made small talk for a moment. Some of them were giving me shit for growing up with Matt and I reminded them that he was their problem now.

When our conversation died down I turned to Matt, focusing back on finding Alex. "Have you seen Alex at all?" I was starting to worry myself thinking of the worst things that could be happening.

"She was here for a little while but I think she was going outside when she left us." I didn't even know there was a backyard, I was preparing for the worst as I walked to the back door. Was she out there with someone? Did she come here to see me or is there someone else she came to see?

I went out back and there was still no sign of Alex anywhere. The backyard was lit by the only light that was next to the door. Most of the backyard was dark and filled with clouds of cigarettes and weed. I took a quick lap around the outside as if I was actually working security at this party and once again no sign of Alex.

I walked back inside, pushed my way through the crowd staying optimistic that I would bump into Alex but never found her. I was starting to psych myself out. I wonder if she left? Did she get a call from an ex like before? Did I miss the one chance I had with her by not talking to her more at the door? All I could think to myself was that it was over. This was our moment and I let it slip right through my fingertips.

I was disoriented, depressed, and disappointed as I made my way back to the front door to reclaim my duty as a bouncer with my brother. Knowing now that Alex was gone took all of the wind out of me. I lost all interest in the party and didn't give two shits about whatever was going on inside. The fresh air was all I wanted. I was desperate to get outside away from all the madness going on. I walked right through the kitchen past my friends, pushed through the living room shoving everyone that was in my way, just to kick open the front door to go back out front.

I kicked the door open aggressively and froze up again. Just as I had a while ago, in damn near the same exact spot when I first saw her. There she was again, waiting for me, smiling just as she was when she first got here. I was speechless, we were speechless and I got lost staring into her eyes. This was our moment. She found the right words to say before me, "I think we must have just missed each other inside. I guess while you went inside looking for me I came out here looking for you."

She smiled that smile, keeping me falling more in love with her. The way she smiled at me, her words of affirmation, quickly washed away all those insecurities and fears I had while I was storming through the house. I couldn't help but smile back knowing that she came here to hang out with me.

"I'm glad you found me, I was worried that you left or something and I missed you. Do you need a drink or anything?" I had to find a way to keep her around. We finally got our moment together. I wouldn't give it any reason to end abruptly. I thought that if she at least had a drink with me I would have that much time to impress her.

"Or would you want to go for a walk or something?" My heart skipped a beat. Did she just ask me to go for a walk with her? I wanted nothing more than to get some alone time with her. She asked softly, she was comforting with her eyes when they locked with mine. There was no way I could say no. I looked at my brother, told him I would be back in a little bit and headed back down Carriage Lane with Alex. After spending the entire day manifesting a chance to have a moment with Alex, it's finally happening.

23

We were just walking, both of us unable to find any words to say initially. All of our friends were at this house party we created and we were walking away from it. That night, neither one of us wanted to be there. All we wanted to do was be with each other without any distractions and see where the hell this would take us. It's something we've both known has been brewing for a while.

I couldn't tell you which way we were walking. I had no idea if we turned left or if we turned right when we got to the end of the street. I was just lost in our conversations. It wasn't that stupid small talk where we caught up on life and class, it was that real intimate conversation. We talked about our heartbreaks, the ones we lost, and how we hope to be more…better than what we had growing up. We both shed some tears, shared a few laughs, and spent the night together just walking around.

Neither one of us bothered to check our phones. Neither of us was worried about what else was going on in the world. This was our moment and neither of us was going to squander it. I'm sure everyone else was fine back at the party. We can catch up with them later. Right now all I wanted to do was to get to know the real Alex. More so than just the person I would always lock eyes with from across the room wondering what could be. Tonight we could find out what could be.

She was more inspiring to me than I imagined her to be. She has walked through a rougher road than she leads on and still stands here strong each and every day. Which is exactly why her beauty shines the brightest in the darkest of rooms. Her smile can instantly turn your worst days into some of your best days. I don't know how it is even possible but I think I'm falling more and more and more in love with her. I am completely infatuated with her.

She asked me a question that I couldn't say yes to quickly enough, "Do you want to come back to my dorm with me? There isn't much we can do but we can at least take our shoes off and watch a movie." I didn't care if we just sat on the floor in her room, I just wanted to keep this night going with her.

"Yes, I'd love to, you just have to lead the way. My decent sense of direction seems to be nonexistent out here." Evidently, we weren't far from her place. This whole time we have been on a direct path from the party back to her dorm like it was her plan the whole time. I followed her step by step, walking side by side with her, admiring her beauty, staring at her every time she looked away. When she would catch me staring at her my face would turn red and all I could do was smile. I knew it that night and there was no going back for me. I was in love.

Walking with her, lost in euphoria, time didn't exist. Before I knew it she was scanning her ID to get into her dorm. The RA was on her laptop working an all-nighter, just asking me to write my name on the guest list. She didn't want to be bothered and neither did we. We both kind of grinned at the paper seeing our names written out together like that gave me chills. It was all about us now.

Alex grabbed me by my hand and pulled me into the elevator with her.. We stepped into the elevator having it all to ourselves. As soon as the door closed we were in there alone. The elevator turned into our own personal kissing booth.

Her lips electrified my heart. She caused it to skip a beat, and beat to her rhythm now. That kiss was and will be the best kiss of my life. Our emotions were honest, or feelings were so pure, it sent me on a high I've never felt before. It was a kiss I have spent years dreaming about, and a lifetime praying for. A kiss I craved more of.

We were standing inches from one another. Our eyes were lost in each other like they had been the entire night and our hands finally found one another's as we started rising together. I didn't believe this moment was happening. I thought this must be a dream.

She is, this whole moment, that kiss, is making me feel things I didn't know I could. All I want is more of this. More of her kisses, more of her laughter, more of her smiles, and more of her kisses. I was keeping it together for a moment until I spoke the words I couldn't hold in any longer. "You're beautiful Alex."

We were silent for a moment. We both needed a second to process all of the feelings we were overcome with that night. "Ah, wait, did I just say that out loud." I thought we were both feeling this moment but her prolonged silence worried me. Maybe the night wasn't going as smoothly as I thought it was.

She didn't let the silence linger after that. She let my hands go so she could grab my cheeks with her hands and kissed me again gently. I kissed her back with the passion of sixteen years and wrapped her tightly in my arms.

"Ding!" The elevator let us know we were on her floor and we holstered our tongues. Our eyes opened and didn't waste a second to find each other. Both of us were smiling bigger than we had all night. We were finally together.

She grabbed my hand and led me to her room, "This way." she said to me as we exited the elevator. Room seven twenty-three. When we got there she pulled out her keys to open the door, turned the lights on inside, and welcomed me to kick off my shoes and relax with her. An offer I could never refuse.

24

The first thing both of us did was take off our shoes. She started claiming she was insecure about the mess and I leaned against the door, too scared to sit down. It was a two-person dorm she shared with a roommate the school gave her. Aside from their beds, they only had enough space for each of them to have a bureau and shared a couch. The place was small, and we were surrounded by cinder block walls that made it feel more like a jail cell than a college.

Personally I had no issue with the setup. All I cared about was being there with her. I didn't know where to sit, overthinking the whole thing. If I sat on the wrong bed I'd be too far from her. If I sat on the couch would I be implying I want to stay in the friend zone? I figured my safest move was to wait until she sat down before I did. At least that way I can sit next to her.

"Would you like a glass of wine, and by glass I mean a solo cup because I don't have any wine glasses here?" She asked me knowing damn well it didn't matter. She was already pulling out two solos from under her roommate's bed and a bottle of white wine from under hers and filled our cups. She handed one to me, put the wine back, and grabbed hers from the top of her bureau. "My roommate went home for the weekend so we can sit on the couch if you want. It's hers but she won't care."

"That's perfect." She led the way and sat down on the couch first. I followed right behind, put my drink on the ground next to my feet, and planted myself right next to her. Aside from when I ate dinner in the jungle that they call McKinley, this was the only other time I've been able to sit down all day long.

I realized that was a mistake immediately. As soon as I leaned back onto the couch the entire world started spinning around me like in a tornado. It was like all the alcohol I had consumed throughout the day was waiting for this moment to hit me at once like a ton of bricks. I couldn't even close my eyes to blink without feeling the world whirling around me.

She leaned her head on my shoulder to rest after the long day we both had. All I wanted to do was lay mine on hers while we spent the rest of the night together. It would be a perfect end to a perfect day. Unfortunately the alcohol had other plans for me. With her head on my shoulder I had to hold my breath to keep myself from puking all over her.

I was faced with the spins severely and there was nothing I could do about it. It didn't matter if I drank a gallon of water or ate a twenty-piece nugget from McDonald's; I was down bad. I had to keep my feet planted on the ground as I sat on the couch wishing for everything to stop spinning. I felt like I was stuck inside one of those spinny roller coaster rides they have at carnivals that gives out ponchos to the people watching so they don't get covered in puke. I was on the roller coaster with a full stomach of the devil's juice ready to vomit. She wasn't giving one of those ponchos. I couldn't hurl all over her.

I took a deep breath and swallowed whatever was working its way back up my esophagus. I couldn't ruin our one moment together by puking in her apartment. When she heard me gulp down my "saliva" she picked her head up from my shoulder and looked at me with the same eyes she had in the elevator. At that point, for me, instinct took over. I couched to clear my throat, took a swig of my wine to clear my puke breath, and closed my eyes as I went in for another kiss.

As soon as my eyes closed my stomach started turning and the world started spinning again. With our lips locked together and her hands on my thighs, I couldn't keep my eyes closed any longer. I needed to see for myself that everything around us was stationary and confirm with my own eyes that the world wasn't spinning rapidly beneath my feet. I kept my lips on hers refusing to let our moment end because I felt nauseous. Nor did I ever want to stop kissing her. I've been waiting for this kiss for most of my life. I wasn't going to cut it short, even if I had to keep opening my eyes every few seconds to keep my stomach at ease.

We were kissing long enough to where I would normally put a move on her and the kissing would have turned into something more. There was no way I would be that smooth that night. I just couldn't focus on anything more than kissing her lips and keeping my puke down in my stomach. Everything else was out of my control. As much as I wanted more I knew I wasn't ready for it.

I think Alex could sense that I was a little off my game and claimed the reins. She pushed me back onto the couch and told me to relax as she sat on top of me. She pulled off my shirt while I was ripping off my socks, and her lips left mine as soon as my shirt slid over my lips.

They found a new place to kiss, touching every inch of my neck. I took that moment to take a deep breath and swallow deeper what was anything that was percolating. Her lips slid down my chest, causing every hair on my body to reach for the stars, leaving me covered in goosebumps. When she got to my stomach she took a deep breath to pause to look up at me to smile.

I found nirvana. That was it. The feelings she was igniting inside my heart were something I had never felt before. She was causing my eyes to roll back in my head. Her soft lips, her warm tongue, and her gentle touch had my heart skipping beats. With everything that I had going on inside my body right now, it was taking everything in me not to make a run for the bathroom and keep this moment from ending.

She unbuckled my pants and shifted her whole body lower on me while she pulled my pants off. I sighed loudly, completely vulnerable. I wasn't sure if it was because she was sending me on this high that I'd never had before or if it was because I was fucked up. My head was spinning faster than any rollercoaster ride you could go on. I was scared to close my eyes for a second, worried that if I did, I wouldn't be able to keep my puke down any longer. But I didn't want it to stop. This was all I wanted but I was way too fucked up to enjoy it the way I've always wanted to.

25

Now all I could think about was that I drank too much and tarnished our night. I won't be able to get myself to do anything more than what we're doing now. The little voice inside me was yelling saying, "You've waited your whole life for this and this is how you spend it?" All I've ever wanted to do was to give her the night both of us have always dreamt about. A night that would sling-shot our lives into the dreams we always knew we shared.

She was making all the moves I couldn't, causing my world to circle around me faster and faster. She had her hands on my chest wanting all of me just as I wanted all of her. I just couldn't do anything to make it happen. The only thing I could focus on was not puking. I lay there staring at the ceiling counting the blades as they spun around to distract my mind from anything else but the alcohol regurgitating in my stomach.

I've been lost in euphoria ever since she smiled at me back at the party. It killed me inside that I now, of all times, wasn't able to do anything to help ignite the spark we've had burning for years now. She was doing everything she could to light the fire, rubbing the log, blowing on it to give it oxygen, finding any way to get it started and couldn't. An issue I never encountered before but as soon as it was happening I knew what I had…"Whiskey Dick."

It was like the two of us had the same revelation. She stopped what she was doing and sincerely asked me, "Is everything okay? Am I doing something wrong?" Hearing her the disappointment in her voice crushed me. This wasn't her fault. Everything we just had going for us came to a halting stop because of me.

I had no idea this would have been the repercussions of drinking far too much all day long. Never have I ever had this happen to me before. I was ashamed of myself that I let the one moment we finally had together crumble because of me. I was disappointed seeing that discouraged look she had in her eyes and it took my soul from me. It was nothing like the way she was glowing while she was staring into my eyes while walking around campus.

"I'm sorry Alex. I swear it's not you. I haven't been able to stop thinking about you since I saw you at the tailgate earlier today. I've been waiting all my life for this moment with you..." I never thought things would be going this well. Paired with the absurd amount of alcohol I consumed earlier has caught up to me. I knew there was going to be a curveball at some point. Things were going too perfectly and this was the bump in our road.

I ran out of words to say. Things were so perfect today. Moments ago we were so high we were floating with the clouds and now it feels like we've fallen lower than we've ever been. Rock Bottom. I was remorseful, this whole thing was my fault. I fucking blew it. I had to lay my cards out on the table.

"If you don't mind me being honest, maybe it was one mixie too many that's giving me some extra liquid courage or maybe it's because I feel like I've totally blown my chance with you tonight and feel like I got nothing left to lose but I've had a crush on you for as long as I can remember. You're the first girl I ever remember having feelings for and after tonight there's no doubt you're the girl I'll have feelings for until the day I die. You're beautiful you know this, but your true beauty exists under your skin. What makes you so beautiful is who you are as a person and tonight I got to finally meet you as a person and

I'm crushing on you harder and harder the longer we spend staring each other's eyes. I can't let my inabilities tonight completely wreck what we have going for us. I couldn't let things end with a sour taste in our mouths and misery in our hearts. There was no way I was going to let this night end without telling you exactly how I feel about you. I think I love you, Alex."

She sat there on the couch while I sat across from her, staring at her hands and processing my perseverating soliloquy. The concerning amount of silence paired with the spins I was feeling was brewing up a storm in my stomach that I couldn't keep down. If I had any chance to keep it down I needed to stand up. When I had both my feet planted on solid ground, the world slowed down. I stood there in the middle of her room patiently waiting for her to speak. I had nothing else to say. I poured my heart out for someone I loved for the first time in my life and was completely vulnerable. My feelings were out there, I said them, and there was no taking them back now. I had no control over what happened next. The rest was up to her.

I could feel her staring at me but I couldn't get myself to look up. Not until she said something. The silence felt like it was going to last an eternity. I didn't even entertain the little voice inside talking in my head. This was the worst case scenario. I didn't need that to make it worse. I just stood there staring at the floor, too terrified to see the look in her eyes. I was too disheartened.

Then she sprang from the couch right towards me to wrap her arms around me for a hug. I heard the little voice inside me yelling, "This is exactly how friends hug each other." I heard it that time thinking to myself that I truly did blow things between her and me. I convinced myself that I got friend zoned and that's all we'll ever be... just friends. She'll just be my great white buffalo. The little voice inside of me has been right all day long.

But that wasn't the case. She pulled her head from my chest and looked into my eyes, glowing once again. Her eyes were sparkling; she wrapped her arms around me tighter, and it felt nothing like the rock bottom we were just sitting in. This was even different from the way she was smiling on our walk, or back in the elevator after kissing for the first time. This time she was staring at me just as googly-eyed as I was. We were in love with each other.

At that moment time stopped for us, the spins disappeared, and It was just her and I together lost in the moment. Her hands were around my neck and mine were wrapped around her waist with our lips slowly, inching their way closer and closer to one another. Finally, I couldn't wait any longer, built up enough testicular fortitude, and went for it. I closed my eyes to kiss her, figuring "Fuck what that little voice was saying. We could never be just friends.

26

It was the best kiss of my life, topping the one we had just shared in the elevator. She kept on kissing me back and I didn't fight her. Our eyes were closed, her hands moved up to my face while mine were still on her hips pulling her in closer, and the world stopped spinning. I never wanted that moment to end. I was in love with her and never wanted to let her go.

The second our lips left each other's was just to breathe so we could stay alive. Simultaneously as her lips left mine my eyes flipped open wondering where her lips went. Seeing her beaming while she caught her breath was heaven to me. There isn't anything that I'd rather open my eyes to see. She is perfect.

With her lips away from mine and her fingers abandoning my skin my face was turning red and becoming hot again. I looked like I was back in middle school getting embarrassed in front of the whole class. I mean I've known she is beautiful, I know we shared something special, but like this. I never thought I would be in love like this. I never thought we would be finding something as real as this. There's no way this can actually be happening to us!

It's been such a long time coming that just one night like this won't make me a believer, but it will damn sure get me listening to my heart. We've always connected and vibed well with each other, but this was like all of my dreams were coming true right before our eyes. This must be a dream, "Alex, do you really like me too?" I know how pathetic it was of me to ask her but I had just opened up my heart. I desperately craved some words of affirmation. A kiss wasn't enough for me that night.

It may have been ten minutes later but she gathered all the words she wanted to say, looking me in the eyes, "I didn't know you felt that way about me." Was this whole thing a misunderstanding? Looking into her eyes, seeing the love in her eyes, she seemed to be oblivious to my feelings for her this whole time.

That's what baffled me most, how could she not know that I have been crushing on her for essentially my entire life? "Come on Alex. You're saying you had no idea I've had this crush on you this whole time?" She has to be messing with me.

Everyone else in our town seemed to know that I had this crush on her, how did no one tell her?

She wasn't believing me. She hit me with that look she has given me all of our life when she's tired of hearing my BS. "I mean yeah. I thought you liked me when we were little but I just thought you thought of us as just friends now."

Just friends. It may be the worst pairing of words I could ever hear her say while talking about us. This whole time she thought I had friendzoned her, so she friendzoned me. Things were adding up now. That's why we never actually gave each other a real chance. We both thought we'd been friendzoned like some classic Shakespeare plot twist and never got a chance to give love a real try.

There was no way I could ever just be friends with her. I've spent my whole life biting my tongue with all things I've wanted to say to her and I couldn't do it anymore. Just friends, no way, it will always be more than that to me.

"I've never thought of you as just a friend. I have loved our friendship, don't get it twisted, but to me, that's only been the foundation for who you and I can be. I think we have so many floors yet to be built, so many roofs to shatter, being just friends can't be the end of our story. It can't be. We've just

162

always kind of been that right thing, just poor timing for twenty years now. Tonight's the first time we've actually had a chance to hang out together. It has to either be the start of something new or the end of everything we could be."

"It has been weird, like every time you're single I have a boyfriend, and every time I've been single you've had a girlfriend and it's just always been shitty timing." She kept her eye contact with me continuing on "Can I be honest?"

I had no idea what she was going to say next but I needed to hear what she had to say more than I needed to breathe, "Of course you can."

"I just feel like our timing has just been off by that much..." She looked down at our hands holding each others, took a deep breath, and then began again, "...And right now it just finally feels right. I mean look at us here together. It's the first time both of us have been single at the same time, and you spent the past couple hours getting to know me more, asking me things no one else ever has. That has to account for something right?" She grabbed my hands tighter and kept on staring into my eyes and I could see she had more to say. "I really like you Tyler. I've kind of always been annoyed or I guess jealous that you've wasted all your time with those girls. All I've ever wanted was to be that girl for you." She lost her train of thought, but our eyes never left each other. They were speaking all the words we couldn't find to say.

I never thought she felt the same way about me. How would I? We never talked like that, we never expressed our feelings before, how would we know we felt the same way? We could never talk about that stuff, we always had someone else to do that shit with. I had nothing smooth to say back, nothing witty, just honesty, "Alex you have no idea how long I've been dreaming about hearing you say that. I just never thought, I can't believe... Alex I just..."

Alex cut me off before I could continue. My mind was racing faster than I could speak. "Do you want to lay down?"

I have to be dreaming. "Do you mind?" I know she offered but I couldn't believe it, did she just ask me to lay next to her? There wasn't anywhere else I wanted to be. Not because I didn't have anywhere else to go or because I was in the middle of a campus with no sense of direction and no telling that any of my friends were still awake. I needed this, more than just a place to sleep, I needed this for me, for us. I just didn't want to intrude by staying over.

"Of course not, that's why I'm asking you. I don't really like sleeping alone either and since my roommate is gone I'd love your company." She was smoother with her words than I was and it prevented me from ever saying no to her.

I followed her to her bed, laying down next to her, as she pulled the covers off her bed tucking myself in right next to her. Still battling the spins, staring at the ceiling praying once again that I would never have to wake up from this dream, as the world spiraled around me.

A few moments later she rolled over to rest her head on my chest. Neither of us said anything, we both were enjoying the moment, refusing to say a word, fighting to itch our noses, rather spending our time holding each other.

"I don't mind keeping you company any time you need it" It was all I had to say. Neither of us had anything left to say. Just being there together seemed to be all both of us could ask for. We just laid there together. I was rubbing her back, while she was rubbing my chest until we passed out in her bed.

27

That was one of the few mornings in my life I didn't wake up as the sun was rising. I had no idea what time it was when I woke up. I was facing the window above her roommate's bed, the sun was blinding me, as she laid sound asleep behind me unfazed by the sun. I woke up ready to explode like a volcano. I was in dire need of a bathroom. I wasn't able to squeeze out one last piss before bed and I'm dealing with the repercussions of it now. Always pee before bed. I had to stealthily creep out of the bed, put my jeans on with my woody who finally got his blood flowing, and race up one floor to find the guys bathroom before I just pissed my pants.

I was barely keeping my feet. I was still a little drunk from last night. I had to lean on the hallway walls to help me stand upright looking for the bathroom door. I saw the sign ahead of me and pushed through the bathroom door. I barely made it to the stall to piss. I didn't even have enough time to unbutton my pants before it started coming out. The first couple drops fell on the seat before I could get my stream into the toilet. I had to lean against the wall to find the right angle to shoot my stream.

Thirty-seven seconds later I pulled up my pants and faced myself in the mirror. Before I could even wash my hands I had to see myself. It wasn't over yet. She let me stay over. That means there's still a chance that I haven't completely blown it yet. I splashed some water on my face to help me wake up, hoping it would make me feel better this morning. It did nothing. I couldn't shake the feeling it gave when I saw the look of disappointment on her face. There was no way I was going to waste our first morning together dwelling on it. It was still our time.

Someone had left their toothpaste sitting on the counter while they were in the shower, so I squeezed some of it onto my finger, and gave myself a little brush before I headed back. I needed a fresh start to the day and I figured that something was better than nothing to help fight my morning breath before I headed back to her room.

She was still sleeping, exactly how I left her. I moved slowly and softly like a thief, sneaking to get under the covers ensuring I wasn't going to wake her up. I felt terrible, like I got hit by a bus. My head was pounding, but laying next to her was the perfect remedy to help me survive that morning. I would have loved to sleep for another couple hours with her before I had to get back to that whole life thing. I wanted to stay lost in this dream with her forever.

I snuck into bed next to her without her knowing and curled myself up back under the covers hating the world. I was just starting to drift out and falling asleep, when I felt her roll over onto me. Her sweet voice is the best alarm clock you can have, "Good morning Tyler, how are you feeling today?" She woke up smiling and somehow was looking more beautiful in the morning light. Significantly better than me. She is the epitome of why they call it beauty sleep. She woke up more beautiful, more attractive, more elegant, than she did all day yesterday.

"Honestly this may be the worst I've ever felt physically but I'm feeling incredibly better waking up next to you,"

She laughed, as she always does when she gets compliments. It's like she never believes them when people say them. Which was perfect because I had no issue reminding her everyday. Waking up next to her, looking into her eyes, telling her how beautiful she is is exactly how I want to spend all of my mornings. Her smile rapidly healed me from my hangover. She rolled over on top of me and rested her head on my chest paralyzing me, just like she did last night. Still this morning, even after waking up next to her, I couldn't believe this was truly happening.

There was this line from the movie "No Strings Attached" that has always stuck with me; "It's not about who you want to spend Saturday night with. It's about who you want to wake up next to on Sunday morning and spend the entire day with." I finally got to wake up on a Sunday morning next to the girl of my dreams. A girl I actually wanted to wake up next to. The girl I wanted to spend the rest of my life waking up next to.

Then she snapped reality back into our world with one question. "What time do you leave today?" Everything I came here, I found, and now I had to leave it all here. That hit me harder than the hangover. I didn't want to leave her, we've only just lit our fire. I wasn't ready to let it end. Not yet.

"Honestly I have no clue, my phone is over there charging. My brother drove, so whenever he's ready I guess."

"So you have some time this morning? We can hang out for a little?" Nor was she ready to let our moment end.

"I mean they probably think I'm still sleeping right now. My phone has been dead, I haven't answered them. My mom would kill my brother if he left without me." We just smiled at each other. We were both sitting up now, staring at each other all googly-eyed, floating on cloud nine together.

"Perfect." She grabbed my face with her hands and kissed me again softly. It was at that moment I was glad I got some toothpaste in my mouth. Her morning breath was irrelevant to me, all I cared about was kissing her. I was vitally craving another kiss from her. As soon as she woke up, all I could think about was feeling her lips on mine again. Then one kiss turned to two, and all of a sudden one thing led to another and our hands fell all over one just like they did last night. The only difference was I could kiss her back that morning.

We spent our entire morning together sharing all of the emotions we couldn't express last night. Her lips were on mine, my fingers were scratching her back, and we were breathing as one.

Our eyes never left each other that morning, not until we made up for the night before.

All I could do was lay there. She rolled off from on top of me to rest her head on my chest. We were silent for a while both unable to separate this dream from reality. I laid there rubbing her back thinking about her eyes and how they're my favorite sight in the whole world, and now for more definitive reasons than ever.

She picked herself up from my chest and leaned on the wall in the corner of the bed finding my eyes to stare into again. I sat up in her bed to be face-to-face with her. We were still silent. I could see it in her eyes that she had something she needed to say and waited patiently for her to find the words to say. "I really like you Tyler. Like more than I have ever liked anyone. I really want to do this thing with you. I've been wanting to do this with you for a while now and I want to give it a try. That is, if you want to?"

Did she just ask me if I wanted to be with her? There's no way this was real life. The hangover I initially felt this morning was non-existent. I was filled with an overfluxation of emotions. Emotions I never thought I would ever feel before. I was feeling happy, excited, scared, and in love all at once. I wanted to run to her but was scared of what would happen and it made me feel like I was going to puke. Between the alcohol from the night before and the butterflies she released in my stomach, I couldn't tell you what was making my stomach sick, but something was brewing there.

This has been everything I have ever dreamt about. The only thing I've ever wanted in my life was to find that real love and with her, I've finally found it. All of my dreams were right there, tangibly, right in front of me. I took every second I could before answering her to find the right words to say to her to ensure I wouldn't ruin this moment any more than I did last night.

I had nothing smooth to say. All I had to say was my true feelings, "I love you Alex. I've been trying to play this game of life with you for a while now and it feels like this is our chance. I just never knew you felt the same way about me. I want to be by your side Alex... all the time. I really like you." I ran out of words when she started beaming her smile back at me. It was all the words I could find inside my brain to say.

She leaned over to hug me with all of the love that had built up inside of her and causing us to fall back into the bed. She was lying on me again rubbing my chest while I laid under her rubbing her back thinking there was no way this could be happening. It was a moment I never wanted to end.

28

I didn't want our time to end. I prolonged looking at my phone as long as I could just to get another few seconds with her. I knew Steven and my brother were probably wondering where I was and waiting for me so we could leave but I wasn't ready. I was lost in that moment. At that moment I was truly and purely happy all because of her. It was nirvana. I hated knowing that it was time for our moment to end.

For a second I contemplated calling out of work on Monday just to spend another night with her. I didn't want this to end because I had to go back home. My home was with her and I never wanted to leave. Not without her holding my hand.

I sat up from the bed rolling out from under her having to come back to reality. In the middle of my sigh of sorrow she asked me to check the time and that's when I knew it was time for me to go. I had four missed calls, ten texts, and two missed Facetime from my brother looking for me. Clearly, they were ready to leave.

"It's almost twelve. I'm sorry Alex, all I want to do is to waste away this Sunday with you. We've finally been able to hang out and I hate that it has to so suddenly. I'm serious about you, like all of this. I want to give what we've been feeling for years now a real chance."

She pulled herself over to where I was sitting on the bed and kissed me on the cheek for reassurance, "I want to do this with you." Then she kissed me on the lips and said, "Let's do this for real. You know, you and I."

I couldn't see it but I could feel my face turning red and blushing once again. Hearing her reiterate how she felt about me was beyond words of affirmation. They were my dreams come true. I wanted to hear it on repeat the whole way home. "I'll talk to you later Alex." I had to steal one more kiss from her before I got up from the bed to leave her. Before I opened the door to leave, after I tied my shoes, I went back to her sitting in bed and kissed her once more before I had to go. I was barely out of the door and was already thinking about the next time I'd see her.

I left her dorm and promptly called my brother back before I even got a chance to hit the button for the elevator. "Hey where are you?" was all he asked when he answered. I could tell that he just wanted to get out of here and go back home. He didn't even say hi.

"I'm leaving the dorms now, would you want to come get me?" I had no idea where I was. There are like twenty-something dorms around campus. All I knew was whatever was out in front of the door I was standing. It had a rotary set up for student drop-offs and a bike rack that was just barely sheltered from the rain. A poorly set up section of the campus if you ask me.

Regardless it was enough context clues for my brother to know exactly where I was. "Okay, we'll be right there. You're all ready to go right?"

"Yeah, I could just use like a muffin or something for breakfast. I'll be good." My body needed something to help me stand a fighting chance against this hangover. An IV would help immensely but I would settle for a muffin and Gatrodade.

"We're stopping now, I'll grab you something, I'll see you in a sec." He hung up the phone before I could say bye. I didn't know where I was but apparently he did. So I just sat on this bench in front of the dorm I described, waiting. I didn't mind waiting, I was still floating on cloud nine. I simply sat there reminiscing on my night. The night where I fell head over toes for Alex.

I never met anyone who I saw three different times, and all three times I was in awe of them. Last night more so than any other she made me fall deeper for her. She showed me a layer of herself I never knew. We talked deeply, became intimate, and shared a night that will be embedded in our brains. I just sat there smiling, thinking about her.

Then this one girl walked by me and I saw the girl wearing the dress she wore out last night. She was covered in stains, her hair was a mess, and I can only imagine how repulsive her morning breath was. I remembered I was out in the Zoo and was able to conclude my experience. The walk of shame. Which, essentially, was exactly what I was doing, except instead of walking I was waiting for a ride.

I started looking around and made a backstory for every girl I saw carrying her heels presumingly walking home from last night. I then noticed this guy, who was way too dressed up for high noon on a Sunday, walking into the dorm I had just left... barefoot. I guess guys can do the walk of shame too. This was college. I saw all these people doing the walk of shame and I just laughed. What a life.

I thought to myself how sad that was to see. I'm out here making my dreams a reality, spending the night with a girl I have loved forever, while all these people have wasted last night on someone they didn't care to wake up next to. I'm more of a who do you want to wake up next to on a Sunday morning kind of guy. It was still surreal to believe that I had a night with Alex. I never thought I would get my chance with her but I'm sure as hell glad I did.

29

My phone started ringing, "Hey I'm pulling up now where are you?" David had just pulled up on campus. "Oh wait, I see you, I'll be right there." and hung up again before I could say anything.

He pulled up to me, giving me door-to-door access. I jumped in the back seat of his car with him and Steven in the front. "How did you know where I was?" I know damn well how pathetic my description was. How did he find me?

"Well you said you were at the dorms, this is Matt's dorm here." He pointed to the dorm on the other side of the drop-off area. "I figured it was a good place to start. Plus I knew what bike rack you were talking about. I would always say the same thing every time I walked past it." It wasn't until David said it that it clicked. I had no idea I was so close to Matt's dorm. Evidently, it wouldn't have been hard for me to find another place to sleep last night. "Did you not stay at Matt's?" That was my brother, he could see it on my face that I had no idea his dorm was so close to me.

"No actually, I had no idea that's where he lived until right now. I actually spent the night with Alex."

"Wait, you saw Alex last night?" Steven, who got lost at the party last night, had no idea Alex was even there. The only reason why I got a chance to see her last night was because I was working at the door.

"You guys told me you were going for a walk but I assumed you eventually came back to the party." David assumed I found my friends and passed out on their floor. Far from what happened.

"I thought we were going to come back to the party. We said we were going for a walk around the block, but things went well. Like real well. Like we were cool before and always hit it off, but last night we took it to a whole nother level. We had a good time together. I guess that is the simplest way to put it." I knew what I wanted to say to them but the more I started thinking about last night the more I digressed to just talking about her. She was still leaving me speechless. "It was far more than I thought it would be, I guess."

"Hell yeah man, that's awesome. I know you were hoping to see her all day, I love that things went well for you guys." Steven was proud of me. He knew what she had meant to me and loved that it became something real.

"Did you guys hang out all night or did you guys hook up?" We're guys after all, David asked but I'm sure Steven was just as curious wondering how well did my night actually went. Just as I would have asked if the roles were reversed.

I paused for a moment to figure out my response, "We did... this morning."

"Wait, this morning?"

It was a vague answer and naturally David needed more detail. So I gave it to them, "Ahh well last night, I think I drank too much. I had whiskey dick. I wasn't able to do anything." I had no problem being honest with them. They were my brothers. I just couldn't tell which moment was more embarrassing; finding out I had whiskey dick last night with the girl I've spent my whole life dreaming about or telling my brothers that I couldn't get myself hard with the girl I've had the biggest crush on for the entirety of my life.

They enjoyed my story and laughed all the way until we got onto the highway. David was the first to stop laughing and actually say something meaningful as opposed to ball-busting, "Ah, I'm sorry that sucks man, we've all been there. I remember one time it happened to me and this girl and she got so mad at me and I was like, no don't be mad this is my fault I'm sorry. I drank too much tonight. She didn't believe me and it hurt their feelings. I still feel bad."

"That was exactly what happened last night. I said the same thing. I said it wasn't her fault. I then had diarrhea of the mouth and proceeded to tell her how I truly felt about her. The best part of the whole night was when she admitted the same thing. She said she has always felt the same way towards me. We spent the entire night talking with each other after my issue. We napped for a couple hours; I brushed my teeth, and now I'm here." We could always speak openly with each other, which is why we are all brothers.

"Well, what about this morning?" David didn't forget what I had said.

"This morning is for her and I. It's been a long time coming and all I can say is that I'm glad it's finally happened." Just after I finished talking about her, her name popped up on my phone and made me smile like a goofy little kid.

David saw my reaction to my text in the rearview mirror and asked, "Alex?"

"Yeah." I smiled and he smiled back, nodding at me as if he was a proud father. He was happy for me. Just as happy for me as I was that I finally made my dreams a reality. For the first time in both her and my lives, we are on the same path. A path we'll be sharing together for the rest of our lives.

Out of all the times our story could have begun, I never thought that our love story would start by pissing on the same tree in the woods. I guess love has a funny way of working itself out, doesn't it? I wouldn't have it any other way.

Printed in the USA
CPSIA information can be obtained
at www.ICGtesting.com
LVHW021546210224
772413LV00066BA/2050

9 789358 314762